Your
Gardening
Year

Your Gardening Year

How to make the most of every month in your garden

CONTENTS

JANUARY

Your garden may appear asleep in January, but there is more going on than you might think. The hardiest vegetables will still be going strong, while evergreens provide reassuring silhouettes in an otherwise bleak landscape. Plus, a sprinkling of snow can bring true magic.

KEY TASKS

- Protect vulnerable plants from severe weather.
- Hoe any germinating weeds.
- Dig over soil, as conditions allow.
- Brush snow off trees, shrubs, and hedges.
- Take hardwood cuttings of trees and shrubs, and root cuttings from perennials.
- Sow some summer bedding under cover.
- Check bulbs being forced.
- Start sowing early vegetable crops under cover.

LAST CHANCE

The weather is at its coldest now, so make sure you've protected container plants from freezing spells and insulated all outside taps against the cold.

AROUND THE GARDEN

Even in the depths of winter, it's surprising how much you can do to prepare for the year ahead.

GENERAL CARE

Nurture the ground

There isn't much you can do outside if the soil is frozen solid—but before you put your feet up indoors, spread well-rotted manure or garden compost over frozen ground. It's a messy job, but a wheelbarrow will make it much easier. Spread the load evenly over the surface; the ground will soon thaw out when the weather improves.

Get to know your soil

It can be disheartening to see plants struggle because they don't suit the soil. Before it's time to start planting in earnest, test your soil for its type and pH—its acidity or alkalinity. Rub some soil between your fingers to get to know its structure: whether it contains a lot of clay, making it heavy and wet, or sand, making it light and dry—or something in between. The perfect balance is known as "loam." Your soil's pH can be tested with ordinary kits stocked by garden centers or online stores; there are plenty available at a variety of costs.

Repair your lawn

Mild and dry January days are ideal for repairing hollows in the lawn. To raise hollow areas, make H-shaped cuts in the lawn with a spade or lawn-edging iron, then carefully push a spade under the turf and roll each half back. Add soil to the exposed area, firm it well, and roll back the turf. Tamp it down with the back of a rake.

TREES, SHRUBS, AND CLIMBERS

Protect newly planted trees and shrubs

Strong winter winds can do significant damage to your trees and shrubs, so make sure you check all the ties and stakes regularly. If they're too loose, a sunken area may develop around the base of the main stem. Too tight, and they may restrict the plant's growth. You can also erect a windbreak to shelter your plants by securing burlap or horticultural fleece to a framework around the plants.

Prune trees to shape

Winter is a good time of year to cut back unwanted growth. Young trees often grow out in all directions, throwing out shoots along the whole length of the trunk. Prune out misplaced stems this month, always making sure that you cut to a junction or the main stem. If you want to grow it into a standard tree with a length of bare trunk, cut back some of the side growths now too. Avoid doing this all at once; instead, do it over two or three years, shortening some branches this year and removing them completely next year.

Keep climbers under control

Some climbers have a habit of working their way into window frames and doors. As growth is a little slower paced in the colder weather, cut climbers back as needed to prevent any expensive damage. Focus on shortening all of the side shoots from the main framework of stems. Keep a close eye on wisteria, ornamental vines, ivies, Virginia creeper, and Boston ivy, as well as climbing hydrangea. Don't forget to prune them away from all gutters on house walls, too.

PERENNIALS, ANNUALS, BULBS, AND BEDDING

Sow sweet peas

Raising your own plants from seed is a thrill that never leaves you, no matter how long you have been gardening. In winter, your options for sowing are a little more limited, but these fragrant cottage-garden favorites will germinate at fairly low temperatures under glass. Sweet peas like a good root run, so it is best to sow them in long sweet pea tubes. Make your own with newspaper rolled into tubes and held together with sticky tape—or keep the cardboard centers from rolls of toilet paper or paper towels. Place the tubes side by side in a seed tray and fill with seed-starting mix. Some seeds, depending on the variety, need soaking overnight to soften the seed coat. Another method is to "chit" the seed—to remove a sliver of the seed coat carefully with a garden or craft knife at the opposite end from the "eye," where the root will start growing. This allows water to penetrate the seeds more easily, hastening germination. There's no need for a propagator—just a cool, light room or sheltered cold frame.

Sow alpine seeds

Winter is also the ideal time to sow alpine seeds outdoors. When sown now, the seeds experience the same period of cold they would in the wild, which is essential for germination in spring. While the seeds are hardy enough to be sown outside, the plants need protection from winter rains. Make them a shelter to keep off the worst of the wet. A piece of glass or clear plastic placed on four sturdy sticks and held down with a large stone is perfect.

Force bulbs

Bring bulbs planted in pots and bowls last autumn inside in batches to give a prolonged flowering display. It's best to bring them in when they have made about an inch of growth, so watch them carefully. Place them in a cool room for a week or two first of all; if it becomes too warm too quickly, they will grow fast, becoming leggy, and produce poor flowers. Water bulbs in bowls without drainage holes carefully or you may overwater them.

TEN-MINUTE TASKS

- **Brush snow** off evergreen hedges before the weight of it splays out the branches.
- **Regularly check bulbs** being stored over the winter. If any have rotted, remove them immediately to stop the disease spreading to other bulbs.
- **Clear weeds** from around plants and cut down any dead stems left for winter interest that are now looking tatty or diseased.

" "

The few plants that dare to flower in January are to be marveled at—and without the distraction of colorful blooms, it's a time to admire the beautiful silhouettes of bare branches and evergreens.

CONTAINERS

Protect pot-grown shrubs

Even the hardiest of pot-grown plants will need protection in the coldest weather: they are more vulnerable to damage from freezing because the roots in the pots are above ground. For some choice plants, it is best to wrap the pots in burlap sacking. For extra protection, wrap straw around the pot and hold it in place with bubble wrap, burlap, or large plastic bags. Grouping the pots together will also give them some mutual protection. Alternatively, if you've got the space, take the plants indoors during bad weather. Even a cold greenhouse, or a

shed with windows, will provide enough protection from all but the most severe frosts. You can wrap the pots, too, to be on the safe side.

Care for winter flowers

Blooms in a winter garden are rare indeed, so if you're lucky enough to have a pot of winter-flowering snowdrops, pansies, or hellebores brightening up your garden, be sure to look after them. Keep the display going into spring by deadheading pansies and cutting back the large hellebores leaves when flowers emerge. As with all container plants, keep them watered too — especially if they are growing at the base of house walls. Here they can be sheltered from rain by the overhang of eaves. It's surprising how dry plants can get in this position, even in winter.

Clean pots and seed trays

Take advantage of this quiet month to give all your pots and seed trays a thorough wash and clean, using a weak solution of detergent and a stiff brush. This will help prevent any diseases or viruses from last year from carrying over to this year's batches of new seedlings.

THE KITCHEN GARDEN

Only the mildest January days will draw you out to your vegetable patch. When you're there, why not sketch out a planting plan for the year?

Dig over your plot

As long as the ground isn't frozen or waterlogged, dig over any empty areas of your plot. This aerates the soil and encourages it to break down into smaller particles. Heavy clay soils may be too wet to work, however. If the soil sticks to your boots when you walk on it, keep off—and leave the digging until next month.

Get ahead with germinating

Anywhere other than the mildest regions will be too cold and wet to sow seeds outdoors this month. Indoors is a different matter, however. Germinating seeds, in a propagator or in a heated greenhouse, will enable you to get a head start on the year.

Make a plan for the year

While your plot is still fairly quiet, think ahead to what you want to grow this year. For inspiration on what to sow, grow, and harvest throughout the year, consult the crop planner on pages 156–159.

HARVEST HIGHLIGHTS

Sprouting broccoli

Hardy varieties of purple sprouting broccoli sown the previous summer should produce a harvest from winter well into spring.

Kale

All kale should be winter-hardy and can be harvested right through the winter months. Varieties such as 'Red Russian', with its pink-colored ribs, can look dramatic on an otherwise empty plot.

Leeks

Harvest leeks just before you need them, as they don't store well. Trim, then wash carefully to remove any soil trapped in between the leaves.

DON'T FORGET

- **Prune** fruit trees, such as apples and pears.
- **Check** and repair nets on winter veggies.
- **Protect** cauliflowers from frost.
- **Force** rhubarb and chicory.

1

2

3

4

5

1 *Helleborus niger* 'Potter's Wheel'

12x18in (30x45cm); Zones 3–8

Its bowl-shaped white flowers and green "eyes," on display from winter to early spring, have earned this hellebore the moniker "Christmas rose."

GROW IT in dappled shade in fertile, preferably heavy, neutral to alkaline soil. For the best displays, trim away old leaves before flowers emerge.

2 *Lonicera* x *purpusii*

6x8ft (2x2.5m); Zones 4–10

Honeysuckle plants bear small clusters of very fragrant white flowers with striking yellow anthers in winter and early spring.

GROW IT in a shrub border or against a warm wall. It needs fertile, well-drained soil in sun or dappled shade.

3 *Prunus* x *subhirtella* 'Autumnalis Rosea'

25x25ft (8x8m); Zones 6–8

This deciduous tree bears small, semi-double pale-pink flowers from late autumn to spring.

GROW IT in fertile, moist, but well-drained soil in sun or light, dappled shade. It needs minimal pruning, in late summer, to remove damaged or badly placed shoots.

4 *Galanthus plicatus* subsp. *byzantinus*

8x3in (20x8cm); Zones 3–9

The snowdrop's nodding, honey-scented, white flowers are one of the first signs that winter is turning into spring.

GROW IT in dappled shade in any fertile garden soil that does not dry out in summer.

5 *Hamamelis* x *intermedia* 'Arnold Promise'

12x12ft (4x4m); Zones 5–8

This slow-growing shrub, also known as witch hazel, adds winter color to the garden with its fragrant, spidery, yellow flowers.

GROW IT in fertile, humus-rich, moisture-retentive, neutral to acid soil in sun or partial shade.

AT THEIR BEST

GET AHEAD

SOW SUMMER-FLOWERING BEDDING PLANTS

On drab January days, the colors of summer might feel far away—but now's the time to sow summer-flowering bedding plants that need a long season to produce flowers. Start seeds under cover, and be sure to make the most of any winter sunshine.

WHY NOT TRY?

You can start sowing a wide range of summer-flowering plants now. Try snapdragons, begonias, geraniums, lobelias, and gazanias.

1.

Sow seeds thinly in clean seed trays or pots. The fine seeds of snapdragons and begonias do not need covering with even the lightest covering of seed-starting mix, while larger seeds should be covered with a thin layer.

2.

Place the seed tray in a propagator that can be maintained at a constant temperature of 70–72°F (21–22°C). On very cold nights some extra heating may be needed.

3.

Position the propagator in the sunniest available spot; a south-facing bench or windowsill is ideal.

4.

Once the seedlings have developed a few pairs of leaves, prick them out into trays or pot them separately.

....
....
....
....
....
....
....
....
....
....
....
....
....
....
....
....
....
....
....
....
....
....

FEBRUARY

February is a month of anticipation: spring is on the doorstep, and new green shoots are readying themselves to burst into bloom. On the mildest days, you can get on with winter pruning and cultivating the soil, but if you're huddled up indoors, why not fill the time with garden planning and preparation?

KEY TASKS

- Feed garden birds in severe weather.
- Apply organic-based fertilizers near the end of the month.
- Ensure plant supports are sound and not too tight before they are hidden by new growth.
- Firm any newly planted trees and shrubs that have been lifted by frost.
- Remove the old stems of herbaceous perennials.
- Start tender perennials into growth under cover.
- Prepare the seedbed for vegetable-seed sowing outdoors.
- Prick out or repot seedlings already growing.

LAST CHANCE

Cut back overgrown shrubs and hedges before the nesting season starts at the end of the month.

AROUND THE GARDEN

February can be very cold, with potentially heavy snow, severe frosts, and lots of rain, but it's not all bad. If you look for it, you'll find ample opportunity to work off the winter blues as your garden begins to come to life.

GENERAL CARE

Give wildlife a helping hand

February is a very hungry month for birds and small mammals. Put out water and food to help them get through until spring—and it may distract them from taking your buds and bulbs, too. This is also a good time to put up bird boxes while trees are still bare. Be aware that birds need a little time to get used to new boxes before they will select them to nest in, though.

Boost borders with fertilizer

Organic fertilizers release their nutrients more slowly than inorganic ones, so apply it now to ensure your plants get the nutrients just as they start into growth in the spring. A sprinkling of naturally derived fertilizer like seaweed meal, pelleted chicken manure, or blood, fish, and bone around the plants will do them a world of good after the long winter. Spread the fertilizer according to the maker's instructions and lightly stir it into the surface of the soil with a hoe or garden fork.

Check all tools and machines

Once the busy gardening season really gets under way, it is maddening to go to the shed and only then remember that your favorite spade has a broken handle. Check the wiring of all electrical appliances for cuts, too. If you are not sure what to do, contact a qualified electrician, or take the tool and cord to your nearest hardware store for advice.

TREES, SHRUBS, AND CLIMBERS

Plant bare-root trees and shrubs

Provided that the soil is not actually frozen, or so wet it sticks to your boots, trees and shrubs you plant this month will get off to a great start. In winter, bare-root plants have an easier ride in soil than plants in containers. Plus, the soil will soon start to warm up, so new roots will help the plant establish quickly.

Give overgrown evergreens a trim

February is a good time to prune back, to the main stems if necessary, any shoots that have become overcrowded or that have grown out awkwardly. If it is a plant that tolerates drastic pruning, such as *Prunus laurocerasus*, *Aucuba japonica*, or *Viburnum tinus*, you could even cut back to ground level. This will encourage strong growth from the base of the shrub. Feed after pruning, preferably with an organic fertilizer, and mulch with organic matter.

Plant new climbers

New climbers are normally supplied grown in containers (as opposed to bare-root), but plant them exactly as you would trees and shrubs (see above). Dig the holes at least 9in (22cm) away from walls and fences so the plant is not in a dry "rain shadow," and guide the young stems up to the permanent framework using temporary supports.

Prune late-flowering shrubs

Shrubs such as *Buddleja davidii* (butterfly bush), *Caryopteris* x *clandonensis*, *Ceanothus* 'Burkwoodii' (deciduous ceanothus), hardy fuchsias, *Lavatera*, and *Leycesteria* (nutmeg bush) flower best on this year's growth, so now is the time to prune them to shape before that growth emerges. It's a terrific job if you've had a bad day, as you can be quite brutal with them! Cut them back hard, leaving one or two buds or shoots on each stem. It might feel as though you're cutting off far too much—but it will get the best show of flowers. Where you want to increase the size of the shrubs, leave a few stems on and prune these lightly. After pruning, give a feed of organic fertilizer and mulch with garden compost or farmyard manure to give them a boost.

PERENNIALS, ANNUALS, BULBS, AND BEDDING

Prepare borders and planting areas

Finish weeding and digging over borders and new planting areas, incorporating organic matter if you can. Cut down any old, dead growth that was left for effect over the winter. The sooner this is done the better, as new shoots will already be emerging from some plants toward the end of the month and they are all too easily damaged.

Protect emerging bulbs

Some delightful dwarf bulbs will flower this month. If they are growing outside, they will benefit from some overhead protection. Use a sheet of glass or acrylic on bricks or a cloche to prevent the flowers from being spoiled by rain and snow. If you use a cloche, you may well be able to bring them into flower a bit earlier, too.

Sow hardy annuals under cover

It's very easy to sow these cheerful plants outside next month, but if you want to get a head start and have earlier flowers, or if you want young plants to fill containers, then sow them under cover now. Their advantage is that they can be planted outdoors without disturbing the root systems—giving them a great start. Keep them watered, and they will germinate in a few days. Plant outside when the seedlings are large enough to handle.

CONTAINERS

Dream up summer planting plans

What plants will you grow in containers and how many? Time spent planning now is well worth it. Besides, it's fun browsing through seed catalogs and dreaming up plant and color combinations. It's all a matter of personal choice and deciding which plants will suit a particular situation, for example sunny or shady spots. If you have space, grow the plants from seed; if you don't have the time for this, garden centers sell young plants now, and if you can bring these in under cover you get a much wider choice by buying early.

Top-dress pot-grown shrubs

Shrubs that have been growing in large pots for several years will benefit from top-dressing with fresh potting mix each year. First, scrape away as much of the old material from the surface as you can—about 1in (2.5cm) is ideal. Then add fresh potting mix with slow-release fertilizer. This will feed the plants over a period of several months, doing away with the chore of feeding them every week or month throughout spring and summer.

TEN-MINUTE TASKS

- **Check that soil** in containers is sufficiently moist, and keep a particularly close eye on evergreens—their foliage can stop rain from getting into the pot, so they're at higher risk of drying out, even in winter.
- **Dig out lawn weeds**, such as clover, one at a time. For weeds with long taproots, such as dandelions, make sure the whole root is removed.
- **Feed herbaceous perennials** with an organic-based fertilizer toward the end of the month, when they'll just be starting into growth.

THE KITCHEN GARDEN

Winter can feel never-ending, but try to refrain from sowing just yet. Instead, focus on getting everything in order for the busier months.

Warm up seedbeds

If you covered areas of your plot with mulch or plastic sheeting last autumn, it should already be dry and relatively warm, ready for your first sowing of seeds next month. To prepare the ground even further, cover with homemade cloches constructed from fleece stretched over wire hoops.

Feed and mulch fruit trees and bushes

Spread a high-potash fertilizer or a naturally derived mixture of blood, fish, and bone or seaweed around the base of your fruit bushes and trees, such as apples, pears, and raspberries. If possible, follow up with a covering layer of rotted-down farmyard manure or compost. This will suppress weeds and help retain moisture. If it isn't damp before mulching, make sure you water it first to keep the moisture in.

Inspect fruit supports

Before spring—and, with it, new growth—starts in earnest, now is a good time to check all stakes, wires, and ties on fruit trees and bushes. Once new foliage appears, it's harder to see what needs attention. Repair any supports that are worn or broken.

"Chit" seed potatoes

Make sure you have bought all your seed potatoes for the year by the end of this month. It's well worth splurging on good-quality tubers, rather than saving and reusing your own, as commercially grown seed potatoes are fairly certain to be free from disease. Spread them all out in egg cartons or seed trays in a cool, light room, where they will sprout shoots—or "chits"—within a few weeks. If the chits look pale and spindly, the room is probably too warm or too dark.

HARVEST HIGHLIGHTS

Celeriac

Lift celeriac as and when you need it. Trim, scrub, and peel it carefully, as the tangle of roots often harbors slugs. Once cleaned up, celeriac is delicious boiled, mashed, or roasted.

Chicory

Forced "chicons" of Belgian or Witloof chicory are a valuable salad crop this month. Grow them as new shoots from roots lifted and replanted last autumn, and blanch them under lightproof covers.

Winter cabbages

Either leave hardy winter cabbages in the ground until you need them, or cut them and bring them indoors for storage. Hang them up in a cool place.

DON'T FORGET

- **Turn** your compost heap.
- **Order** new asparagus crowns.
- **Check** for slugs in cabbages and cauliflowers.
- **Finish** winter pruning fruit trees, such as apples and pears, by the end of this month.
- **Spread compost** or well-rotted manure over your plot. Work it in as you dig or leave it over the surface as a top dressing.

1 *Erica* x *darleyensis* 'Arthur Johnson'

3ftx30in (1mx75cm); Zones 5–7

From midwinter to spring, this low-growing heather adds welcome color to the garden, with its mauve-pink flowers.

GROW IT in an open, sunny site in well-drained acid soil. After flowering, trim then top-dress with leaf mold or compost.

2 *Viburnum tinus*

10x10ft (3x3m); Zones 7–8

This shrub displays clusters of perfumed white flowers in winter, while its glossy leaves are attractive all year.

GROW IT in sun or partial shade in any fertile, moist, but well-drained soil. Trim hedging after flowering. On freestanding specimens, shorten any overlong shoots that spoil the outline.

3 *Euonymus fortunei* 'Silver Queen'

8x5ft (2.5x1.5m); 20ft (6m) if climbing; Zones 5–9

With shiny green leaves with white, often pink-flushed margins, this Silver Queen reigns all year long.

GROW IT in any well-drained soil, ideally in full sun, though it will tolerate light shade. Trim in mid- to late spring.

4 *Camellia* x *williamsii* 'Anticipation'

12x6ft (4x2m); Zones 7–9

This camellia's beautiful, peony-like crimson flowers appear from mid-winter to mid-spring.

GROW IT in humus-rich, lime-free (acid) soil, or in acidic potting mix in pots. It thrives in sun or dappled shade.

5 *Iris* 'Harmony'

6x2in (15x5cm); Zones 7–9

In late winter, this iris's yellow-marked, royal-blue flowers will appear amid a sheaf of narrow leaves.

GROW IT in full sun in rock gardens or containers. Add coarse sand to heavy clay soils to improve drainage.

AT THEIR BEST

GET AHEAD

PREPARE GROUND FOR SOWING GRASS SEED

If you want a new lawn in spring and you haven't dug over the ground yet, now is an excellent time to get it done. By the end of March, the soil will have warmed up enough to give grass seed a flying start.

WHY NOT TRY?

As an alternative to traditional grass seed, sow an annual wildflower seed mix to create a mini-meadow that will attract and support pollinators. Premade seed mixes, including the likes of corncockle, cornflower, corn marigold, and field poppy, are widely available.

1.

Dig over the ground for your lawn, being sure to incorporate organic matter to help retain moisture.

2.

Remove all perennial weeds, large stones, and clods of soil as you see them.

3.

Leave the ground to settle for a couple of weeks.

4.

Level the soil off and rake it down to a fine tilth (a fine, crumbly surface for sowing seeds).

5.

Sow seed when the weather has started getting a little warmer, but before it's so dry that your lawn won't benefit from seasonal rain.

MY GARDEN IN FEBRUARY

....
....
....
....
....
....
....
....
....
....
....
....
....
....
....
....
....
....
....
....

MARCH

March can be cold, but you'll get plenty of bright days, too—especially when the clocks go forward. That extra hour of daylight gives gardeners more time to get everything done—and there's quite a list. But the riot of spring blooms will give plenty of encouragement.

KEY TASKS

- Start mowing lawns regularly, and reseed any bare patches.
- Mulch bare soil in borders.
- Put pond pumps back into the pond, and make sure they're safe.
- Water indoor plants regularly.
- Propagate shrubs by layering.
- Prune shrubs with colorful winter stems.
- Sow hardy annuals where you want them to flower, and sow vegetables outside.

LAST CHANCE

If you want to plant bare-root trees and shrubs, now's your last opportunity until autumn. As the weather gets warmer and foliage develops, they find it harder to retain water, making it more difficult for them to establish.

AROUND THE GARDEN

There is nothing better for clearing out the winter cobwebs than working in the garden on a clear, warm spring day. Luckily, March has plenty to keep you busy.

GENERAL CARE

Look out for pests

As the warmer weather returns, many pests return with it—so keep an eye open for signs of slugs and snails, which can cause damage to plants. An organic solution is to water a tiny nematode onto the soil when the weather warms. Traps are also effective. One of the oldest and best known is the beer trap: a jar sunk into the ground with the lip just above the surface, filled with beer. Opossums, frogs, toads, and some birds also prey on these particular pests, so do what you can to encourage these predators. Lay a flat stone in a border and you will soon notice if a bird is using it as a handy "anvil" on which to smash snail shells.

Mulch bare soil

Weed and tidy bare soil, then mulch it with organic matter like well-rotted farmyard manure, garden compost, or chipped bark. In dry spells, bare soil in borders will very quickly lose water. Covering with a thick layer of organic matter will slow this down and reduce the need to water. This is especially important for young trees, shrubs, and perennials that have been recently planted—and you don't want to let them go short of water in their first year. Mulch will also suppress weeds. Never put mulch on top of dry soil, though: if the soil is dry, water it first. A layer of compost is just as good at keeping water out as sealing it in.

Repair damaged lawn edges

Lawn edges can easily become damaged in summer, and they can even crumble away in places—especially with light, sandy soils. Now is a good time to put things right. Cut out the entire damaged portion of turf and turn it around so the good side now becomes the edge. Fill in the hollow edge with soil and sow it with grass seed. Water and scatter straw over the top to encourage the grass seed to grow, and then you will have a perfect repair.

TREES, SHRUBS, AND CLIMBERS

Layer shrubs to make new plants

Many shrubs, such as hydrangeas and philadelphus, will layer themselves quite easily by forming roots on shoots touching the ground. But for plants that need a little more encouragement, cut into the stem to stimulate root growth and dust the wound with hormone rooting powder before pegging it down. The layered shoot will have formed roots by the following spring, when it can be cut from the parent plant and planted elsewhere.

Transplant shrubs

As the soil starts to warm up, March is a good month to move shrubs. Plants will begin to take up water from the soil now, which will help them reestablish just as they begin to grow. When moving shrubs, take as large of a root ball as you can manage—if it's particularly large and heavy, you might need to enlist help to carry it to its new home. Provide protection from cold winds with a screen of burlap, and be sure to keep it well watered.

Create new hedges

If you've been thinking of establishing a new hedge in your garden, now's your last chance to buy and plant bare-root hedging plants. After March, only container-grown plants will generally be available until autumn, which can make buying in bulk for hedges expensive.

PERENNIALS, ANNUALS, BULBS, AND BEDDING

Support herbaceous perennials

Toward the end of the month, herbaceous perennials will be showing plenty of new growth, but heavy rain or strong winds can do damage to the shoots. Whatever support you use—from twiggy sticks ("peasticks") to canes—it's crucial to stake perennials early in the year so that the plants will look natural as they grow. Don't put it off until the plants flop or are blown around; trying to stake stems that are growing in all directions is a headache best avoided.

Plant summer-flowering bulbs

To guarantee a succession of flowers in summer and into autumn, plant summer-flowering bulbs this month and next in warmer parts of the country. Choose a sunny position in well-drained soil. If you're concerned about frosts, wait until next month to plant the frost-tender bulbs such as gladioli, eucomis, and tigridias.

Harden off hardy annuals sown under cover

Hardy annuals that were sown under cover (see page 22) can now start their journey into the outdoors. Help them acclimatize by putting the plants in a cold frame, top closed, for a few days. Gradually increase ventilation until the lid can be left off or up. This should take about a week or ten days. If a sharp frost is forecast, add insulation, such as horticultural fleece, at night.

TEN-MINUTE TASKS

- **Take cuttings** from dahlia tubers when the shoots are 3–4in (8–10cm) long but before the stems hollow out.
- **Finish pruning** summer-flowering clematis.
- **Protect** the young, tender shoots of delphiniums and hostas from slug damage by putting a physical barrier, such as copper tape, in place.
- **Feed** winter-flowering heathers pruned in February with a high-nitrogen feed.
- **Look out** for germinating weed seedlings and take them out with a hoe.

" "

Spring flowers brighten up the garden in March, while early-flowering cherry trees herald the spectacular displays of blossom to come next month.

CONTAINERS

Plant your pots

Now's the time to put your planning into practice and plant your pots. When it comes to growing plants in containers, let your imagination run wild: small trees, shrubs and climbers, herbaceous perennials, annuals, alpines, and ground-cover plants. The only real rule is to look after them well: don't forget to water, feed, and deadhead them regularly. If you're inclined to forget feeding, try adding a slow-release fertilizer. This works by naturally breaking down and releasing nutrients over time.

Trim and divide herbs

Tidy up perennial herbs growing in pots, such as rosemary and sage, by cutting back old woody growth. This will encourage healthy new stems and leaves to grow in their place. March is also a good month to increase your stocks of chives and mint. Dump any clumps of herbs onto a surface and divide them into smaller groups. Plant these either into the existing pot with rejuvenated soil or into new containers. Water them well. The plants should have a good start and give plenty of new growth.

THE KITCHEN GARDEN

With colder weather now in retreat, outdoor sowing can begin tentatively with potatoes and onions. You can also prepare your seedbeds.

Get seedbeds ready for sowing

As the weather gets warmer, remove fleece or cloches from seedbeds. Rake over the soil, breaking down lumps, until it forms a fine tilth. This is every vegetable gardener's dream: crumbly soil, with no stones or large clods. If it's too dry and dusty, water it. If it sticks to your boots, let it dry out a little.

Feed overwintering crops

Vegetables that have been in the ground over the winter—such as onions, kale, and hardy lettuces—may be a bit worse for wear. Perk them up with a top dressing of blood, fish, and bone meal; chicken manure; or seaweed-based organic fertilizer.

HARVEST HIGHLIGHTS

Spring onions

Your first spring onions of the year should be ready for lifting now, if you sowed seeds last August or September and left them in the ground to overwinter.

Spring cauliflowers

Provided they have survived any severe frosts or very cold weather, hardy, overwintering spring cauliflowers planted outside toward the end of last summer should now be ready to harvest.

Swiss chard

This month you should be picking the first of the year's Swiss chard and perpetual spinach that overwintered from seeds sown last summer.

DON'T FORGET

- **Remove dead leaves** from brassicas to stop mold and downy mildew from spreading.
- **Check for aphids** on all soft fruit bushes.
- **Apply fertilizers** before seeds are sown.

1 *Daphne mezereum*

4x3ft (1.2x1m); Zones 4–7

From late winter until early spring, mezereum's exquisitely perfumed pink flowers cluster on bare branches.

GROW IT in sun or partial shade in slightly alkaline, humus-rich, moist but well-drained soil.

2 *Chaenomeles* x *superba* 'Knap Hill Scarlet'

5x6ft (1.5x2m); Zones 5–9

This spiny-stemmed, deciduous shrub brightens up the early spring garden with large scarlet flowers with golden anthers.

GROW IT in any fertile, well-drained soil in sun or partial shade. It works well for shrub borders, sunny or shaded walls, and hedging.

3 *Corylus avellana* 'Contorta'

15x15ft (5x5m); Zones 4–8

These long catkins add interest to a hazel's contorted branches in late winter and early spring.

GROW IT in any good garden soil in sun or partial shade, ideally at the back of a shrub border. Remove any suckers that grow from the base and prune misplaced shoots in winter.

4 *Primula* Gold-laced Group

10x11in (25x30cm); Zones 5–8

This rosette-forming perennial produces clusters of velvety mahogany-red flowers, each petal with a gold edge.

GROW IT in full or partial shade in moist, fertile, humus-rich neutral to acid soil. It thrives in borders, bedding, containers, rock gardens, or alpine houses.

5 *Hyacinthus orientalis* 'City of Haarlem'

12x3in (30x8cm); Zones 4–8

The hyacinth's sturdy stems arise in spring, bearing dense spikes of highly scented, soft primrose-yellow flowers.

GROW IT in full sun, in fertile, well-drained soil. Plant as spring bedding or in pots indoors.

GET AHEAD

PRUNING ROSE BUSHES AND SHRUBS

If you're dreaming of big, fragrant blooms this year, now's the time to prune your rose bushes and shrubs. Pruning roses builds a healthy framework of shoots that will produce a good display of flowers. Thinning overcrowded growth also allows in light and air, so you're less likely to face problems with pests and diseases. Cuts must be clean, so use a pair of sharp pruners.

GOOD TO KNOW

Never prune ramblers in the spring unless you need to drastically renovate them, as you will lose this year's flowers.

1.

Remove any dead or unhealthy wood. Leaving this on the plant can encourage diseases to invade.

2.

Cut out any shoots that are crossing and rubbing against another. Now the flowering wood can be pruned.

3.

Here, the method varies depending on the rose type, but the key points to remember are: always prune to outward-facing buds; and the harder you prune, the more vigorous the subsequent growth will be.

4.

Finally, mulch around the roses, with well-rotted farmyard manure or a bagged product such as shredded bark.

MY GARDEN IN MARCH

....

....

....

....

....

....

....

....

....

....

....

....

....

....

....

....

....

....

....

....

....

....

APRIL

April is perhaps the most exciting month of the year. The garden suddenly begins to look green and vibrant, and the warmer days and lighter evenings gladden the heart. With all this exuberance, there is a tremendous amount of work to be done, so get out there!

KEY TASKS

- Plant evergreen trees and shrubs.
- Tie in the new shoots of climbers.
- Prune early-flowering shrubs as well as those grown for large or colorful foliage.
- Watch out for slugs and snails.
- Divide perennials, and stake tall-growing ones.
- Sow annual climbers and grasses.
- Keep hoeing to suppress weeds, but always dig perennial weeds right out.
- Sow seed or lay sod for new lawns, and feed established lawns.
- Prick out or repot seedlings—including self-sown seedlings—before they get congested and grow leggy.

LAST CHANCE

With spring in full swing, April is your last chance to plant summer-flowering bulbs and sow sweet peas.

AROUND THE GARDEN

Famous for its showers, April provides ideal growing conditions — which means lots to do in the garden. Make the most of your time outside to keep everything looking neat and prepare for the summer months.

GENERAL CARE

Prepare your borders

Just one morning or afternoon dedicated to small jobs in your garden can make all the difference in its appearance. Lightly fork over the soil, pulling out emerging weeds. Any plants taking up too much space and growing across other plants can be lightly pruned into shape to keep them looking tidy. (Don't be too hard with the pruning, though, or you may cut off all this year's flowers.) Put in plant supports as you go.

Watch the weather

Any gardener knows that weather is a fickle friend — and this month can be especially changeable. April might be renowned for its showers, but that doesn't mean cold snaps are completely off the table, with heavy frosts and even snowy spells infrequent but not unusual. Keep an eye on the forecast and protect tender plants on frosty nights with covers or fleece — even a few sheets of newspaper can make all the difference.

Feed established lawns

Now's the time to feed your lawn. Always follow the manufacturer's instructions. There is no point in putting on a little extra to "speed things up": plants will only take up a certain amount of nutrients, and the excess leaches into the water table and then into streams and rivers.

TREES, SHRUBS, AND CLIMBERS

Remove frost-damaged shoots

Slightly tender evergreen shrubs, such as *Choisya ternata* (Mexican orange blossom), can be damaged by early spring frosts. Remove any affected shoots. If necessary, you can prune back any misplaced stems at the same time. In colder areas, pruning these shrubs is best left until next month in case a late hard frost causes more damage. Stems should always be cut back to a healthy leaf lower down the shoot, or to a stem junction.

Tie in shoots of twiners

Twiners, such as clematis, are growing fast now, so it's an opportune moment to tie in any shoots. With clematis, once it gets ahold of its support it can usually be left to get on with it, especially if growing through other shrubs, but it may need some guidance if it is encroaching too much on other plants.

Prune early-flowering shrubs

Shrubs such as forsythias and chaenomeles put on a terrific show of color in the spring on wood made the preceding summer. When the flowers have died off, it's time to prune them for next year's display. Cut back the flowered shoots to two or three buds from their base. On more established shrubs, cut out about a third of the older growth to the base of the plant. For trained plants, first tie in any stems you need to fill gaps, then prune as above.

Plant container-grown trees and shrubs

Bare-root deciduous stock will no longer be available, but container-grown specimens should be available at any time of the year (though spring and autumn are best for the plants). Water the plant well an hour or two beforehand, then ease the root ball out of the pot. Set it firmly in a generously sized hole so the top of the root ball is level with the ground around it. Work soil down around the sides of the root ball with your fingers, water well again, and mulch around the plant to lock in that precious moisture.

PERENNIALS, ANNUALS, BULBS, AND BEDDING

Thin shoots on perennials

To get top-quality flowers from border plants, it can be well worth thinning out overcrowded shoots. Focus your attention on delphiniums and lupins. Phlox will also put on a bolder show if thinned. Remove about one in three or four of the shoots, depending on crowding.

Sow annual grasses

The delicate foliage and attractive seedheads of annual grasses contrast well with broad-leaved plants in borders. They can be sown outside from now on. Try sowing grasses in drifts as with annual flowers—in drills, so that you can tell them from weed grasses when they germinate. Once they're big enough, transplant them in among plants in the border.

Keep beds neat

By the end of April, spring bedding may be starting to look past its best—but don't let the spring sunshine fool you: summer bedding cannot be planted outdoors safely for a few weeks yet. Do what you can to keep plants neat, instead of pulling them out too early to leave bare ground that weeds will colonize.

Sow more unusual annual climbers

Climbing plants have many practical uses: adding height to a border or hiding ugly buildings or unsightly places like the compost heap. A cheaper and quicker alternative to permanent perennial climbers is to plant annual climbers. Lovely plants to try include *Ipomoea* (morning glory), which has blue or pink flowers; *Cobaea*

DEADHEADING THE LAST DAFFODILS

Daffodils are a welcome burst of color in early spring, but once April gets going, the flowers usually start to die off. Snap them off behind the swollen part. Removing the old flowers diverts the plant's energy into the formation of next year's flower bud within the bulb. For this to happen, the foliage must be left on the plant. Either let it die back completely, or cut it down six weeks after the flowers are over.

scandens, with violet and purple flowers; Chilean glory vine (*Eccremocarpus scaber*), with funnel-shaped red and yellow flowers; and black-eyed Susan (*Thunbergia alata*). Sow the seeds thinly and cover lightly with vermiculite as some of them need light to germinate. They will all need a temperature of around 64°F (18°C).

Repot rooted cuttings

Any cuttings taken from tender perennials last year, and kept on a windowsill or shady part of a greenhouse, can now be repotted, provided they've rooted. Keep them under cover until next month, when you can start hardening them off for planting outdoors.

TEN-MINUTE TASKS

- **Remove** all winter protection from alpine plants and beds toward the end of the month.
- **Tidy up** winter-flowering heathers by removing tatty flowering stems with shears to show off more attractive new growth.
- **Cut back** lavender once the plants approach the size you want them to grow.
- **Check** roses for aphids as their numbers will now be rising.

" "

Walking around the garden on a warm April day, taking in the sights and smells of spring, can really lift your spirits.

CONTAINERS

Prepare containers and pots for summer

To help keep pests and diseases at bay, clean all containers that are to be used for summer bedding displays. Use a weak solution of ordinary household detergent and scrub them thoroughly.

You could also spruce up older, scruffy containers with a multisurface garden paint, perhaps even experimenting with some more unusual shades to enhance summer color schemes. If you're feeling especially creative, give unneeded objects a new lease on life by transforming them into plant pots. From old wheelbarrows and chimneys to a stack of tires or even a colander—just make sure whatever you use has adequate drainage before planting in them.

Plant alpine troughs

Whether you buy a trough or sink, or make your own, April is an ideal month for planting alpines: many are coming into flower now, so you can get an instant effect. The most important point to bear in mind when growing alpines is that they like good drainage, so any container used for these plants must have plenty of drainage holes in the bottom, topped with a 2in (5cm) layer of broken pots or coarse gravel in the bottom to help with drainage. Be sure to fill the container with "alpine mix," which consists of equal parts garden soil, garden compost or coir, and coarse sand. After planting, spread a layer of coarse sand over the surface of the potting mix between the plants. This not only sets off the plants well, but also keeps down weeds and prevents the plants from being splashed with soil in rainy weather.

THE KITCHEN GARDEN

The days are longer and warmer, but resist the temptation to tear open your seed packets and sow outdoors. It's still safest to grow under cover.

Prick out seedlings

Check any seedlings grown in trays or cells. Once they have developed a couple of true leaves, move them into individual pots. This is called "pricking out." Use a dibble or a pencil to lever them very gently out of the soil, taking care not to damage their delicate roots. Always handle seedlings by the leaves, not the stem. Once replanted, they will develop their own root system without crowding or competition from neighbors.

Repot growing plants

Keep an eye on your seedlings growing in pots—tomatoes in particular. If it's still too early to plant them outdoors, they may become "pot-bound" and their roots will be constricted. Worry not: there's an easy fix. Simply repot them in larger pots until they can go out into the ground.

Build cane supports for pole beans

April is a good month to erect supports for beans, as the ground is still soft enough to push in canes or stakes easily. Traditional supports take the form of tripods of double rows crossed over at the top. Use strong canes and thick twine or wire to withstand winds and support the weight at the peak of the harvest.

HARVEST HIGHLIGHTS

Asparagus

Watching the very first asparagus spears of the year pushing their way out of the ground is one of the highlights of April. Start cutting them once they are about the thickness of your index finger—or earlier if you can't wait!

Lettuces

Some lettuce varieties are bred to withstand light frosts. Sown the preceding autumn, and given some protection during the winter, lettuce types like these should be ready to be harvested now.

Arugula

Start picking arugula as soon as the young leaves are about as long as your thumb. Keep picking and they'll keep growing.

DON'T FORGET

- **Harden off** young plants raised indoors. Move them outside on warm days and then back in again at night. Cold frames or cloches are also good halfway houses.
- **Attach brassica collars** if you are planting early summer cauliflowers to protect them against the eggs laid by cabbage root fly.
- **Check for aphids** on all soft fruit bushes, and deal with them before they develop into a major infestation and cause damage.
- **Cover** blossoming nectarines, apricots, and cherries with fleece to protect them from any late frosts.
- **Water** newly planted seedlings regularly. Little and often is better than a deluge once a week. Weed thoroughly, too.

1 *Magnolia stellata*

9x12ft (3x4m); Zones 4–8

Silky buds open in early and mid-spring to reveal star-shaped white flowers, earning it the common name "star magnolia."

GROW IT in moist but well-drained, fertile, humus-rich soil in sun or dappled shade. Keep it sheltered from cold winds and late frosts, which may damage the flowers.

2 *Cytisus* x *praecox* 'Warminster'

4x5ft (1.2x1.5m); Zones 6–9

The arching branches of this evergreen shrub are wreathed in pealike, creamy-yellow flowers in spring.

GROW IT in moderately fertile, well-drained soil in full sun. After flowering, cut back the flowered shoots to buds lower down young wood. Don't cut into old wood.

3 *Fritillaria meleagris*

1ftx3in (30x8cm); Zones 4–8

The bell-shaped flowers in checkered shades of pink, purple, or white give this plant its common name: snake's head fritillary.

GROW IT in fertile, humus-rich, moisture-retentive soil in sun or partial shade. It's suited to rock gardens or naturalized in sod.

4 *Vinca minor*

8in (20cm) tall; spread indefinite; Zone 4–9

This trailing evergreen shrub bears blue-violet—and occasionally pale blue, red-purple, or white—flowers from spring until autumn.

GROW IT in any but the driest soil, ideally on a shady or sunny bank or border. In sun, the soil must be reliably moist.

5 *Pulsatilla vulgaris*

8x8in (20x20cm); Zones 4–8

Nodding, bell-shaped, silky-hairy flowers in shades of pink and purple (or occasionally white) appear in spring.

GROW IT in fertile, sandy, sharply drained soil in sun. It thrives on shallow chalky soils. Pulsatillas dislike being disturbed; so, when planting, choose your site with care.

GET AHEAD

MAKE YOUR OWN COMPOST BIN

Composting is all about recycling the goodness in dead plant material – so making your own compost bin out of recycled materials seems very fitting indeed. It also makes the moment you spread home-made compost for the first time all the more satisfying. Adapt these instructions based on whatever materials you have to spare.

1.

Hammer wooden posts 12in (30cm) into the ground in a square, each 30in (75cm) from the others. Wrap chicken wire around the posts on three sides of the square. Secure with staples.

2.

Construct walls on three sides by sliding several layers of flattened cardboard between the chicken wire and the posts.

3.

Start filling the bin with old plant material and vegetable kitchen waste. Don't compost any diseased material.

4.

Water from time to time so that it stays damp, but cover it to keep off heavy rain and to allow heat to build up.

5.

After a year or so, you should have a pile of rich, dark, sweet-smelling compost.

MY GARDEN IN APRIL

MAY

Make the most of May's warmer weather to start getting ready for summer. Your garden should be approaching its best, with colorful spring bedding and trees in full leaf. Plus, the flower-show season will give you even more ideas and inspiration for the coming months.

KEY TASKS

- Protect tender plants from late frosts.
- Trim any formal hedging lightly.
- Protect young plants from slugs and snails.
- Clear out spring bedding to make space for summer bedding plants.
- Move tender plants outside now for the summer.
- Sow and plant tender vegetables outdoors, and continue successional sowing of vegetables.
- Ventilate greenhouses or conservatories during warmer weather.

LAST CHANCE

If you're still planning to plant evergreen shrubs, sow grass seed, or lay new sod, do so now before the conditions become too dry.

AROUND THE GARDEN

With the freshness of spring and the promise of summer, May is a particularly lovely month to spend in the garden — and there's plenty to be getting on with.

GENERAL CARE

Preparing for night frosts

Even though daytime temperatures should now be mild, night frosts are not uncommon this month, especially after clear, bright days. Keep a sheet of horticultural fleece or even some old newspapers handy to cover any plants that are vulnerable to frost if night temperatures are forecast to fall.

Dealing with weeds

Hoe bare ground to keep down weeds as they germinate. Weeds are more easily killed off at this stage, rather than leaving them until they get bigger, as they won't have the chance to set seeds that will be spread around the garden. Hoe on dry, sunny days and the weed seedlings can be left on the surface of the ground to dry out and shrivel up in the sun.

Start mowing the lawn

Now that the grass is growing well, mow established lawns once a week. Set your lawnmower to cut the grass to 3in (7.5cm) or higher. A deep, lush lawn resists weeds without the use of herbicides. Cutting the grass too short will make the grass turn yellow and cause bare patches to develop, allowing weeds and moss to establish — and it looks unsightly, too.

TREES, SHRUBS, AND CLIMBERS

Water newly planted trees and shrubs

A few days of sunny weather accompanied by drying winds in May will dry out the soil surprisingly quickly, so water newly planted trees and shrubs regularly. You may need to water them on a daily basis. You can also apply an organic mulch, such as rotted manure or garden compost, around the base to retain water and help new, growing roots.

Prune early-flowering shrubs

The likes of *Kerria japonica* and *Spiraea* 'Arguta' will finish flowering about now on wood produced the previous year. For kerria, prune all the shoots that have produced flowers back to young side shoots lower down, and remove underground suckers if the shrub seems to be encroaching on other plants. Likewise, prune the flowered shoots of *Spiraea* 'Arguta' back to buds or shoots lower down on the shrub. Then cut out about one in three of the older stems completely to the ground; this encourages new growth from the base, keeping the plant vigorous and healthy.

PRUNING CLEMATIS

The vigorous climber *Clematis montana* should be pruned after flowering. The amount of pruning will depend on where it is growing. Not much will be needed if it is scrambling through trees or up a wall, but in more confined spaces some pruning will be necessary to keep it from taking over the whole garden. Pruning is easy, although the untangling can be tricky; all you have to do is prune out any dead or diseased wood and cut the remaining stems back as far as you need to. This encourages young growth to take place and flowers to come next spring.

PERENNIALS, ANNUALS, BULBS, AND BEDDING

Take cuttings from tender perennials

Cuttings taken now from the likes of argyranthemums, pelargoniums, and fuchsias will provide plants for flowering well into autumn, but you must have somewhere frost-free to raise them until all danger of frost has passed. Trim the cutting immediately below a leaf joint and dip the end in hormone rooting solution. Put the cuttings into pots containing moist seed-starting mix. Place a plastic bag over the pot, and put it on a shady windowsill so that they don't dry out. They will root in three to four weeks, when they can be repotted so that they are ready to plant outdoors in June.

Thin out hardy annuals

If they are not thinned, annuals will become leggy and won't flower well. Thin out to leave one seedling at least every 6in (15cm). The taller the plants, the more space they need. Simply choose the one you want to keep and pinch out the others. Measure the gap to the next one, and do the same until the job is done. Most hardy annuals don't transplant well when they grow taller, so if you thin them out as soon as the seedlings can be handled, they can be transplanted to fill gaps, or you can put them in other parts of the garden.

Sow half-hardy and hardy annuals

The likes of clarkia, calendula, and candytuft (*Iberis*) can all be sown early this month to produce flowers in late summer and autumn.

TEN-MINUTE TASKS

- **Prune evergreens** to remove any frost damage, and tidy any wayward shoots.
- **Check roses** for aphids, and take action to eliminate them.
- **Deadhead** spring-flowering bulbs that are still going. Snap off tulip heads and leave the stalks. Leave the foliage intact for at least six weeks after the last flower to help replenish the bulb.

" "

Ornamental borders will be brimming with colorful late-spring flowers, the sound of birdsong will fill the garden, and insects will be pollinating flowers.

CONTAINERS

Remove spring bedding

Make room for summer bedding in pots by discarding the spring bedding. It's also worth removing some of the old potting mix if it has been in the container since last year and adding fresh peat-free potting mix to give the new plants the best possible chance to thrive.

Water and feed containers

As the weather starts to get warmer, watering containers can become a daily or twice-daily task—especially for hanging baskets, which are prone to drying out. Remember to feed plants too; a high-potash feed is best for the production of flowers and a prolonged display.

Watch out for common pests

These can wreak havoc when they multiply within the close confines of a container. To avoid introducing them when you add new plants, check all prospective purchases carefully for aphids, red spider mites, whitefly, and mealybugs. Reject any infested plants. Avoiding problems is easier than treating an infestation.

Move tender perennials and shrubs outside

In most regions, these plants can be moved outside sometime in May, but you may want to wait until early June in northern areas. The sooner these plants can be put outside the better: the fresh air and rain after their prolonged period indoors will do them a world of good. Larger-leaved shrubs, such as bay laurel, can have their leaves wiped with a damp cloth. This will remove dust and dirt accumulated indoors. Be sure to keep up with watering and feeding, too.

THE KITCHEN GARDEN

With longer, warmer days, May often brings a foretaste of summer. Many spring crops will be at their peak this month.

Tidy up fruit bushes and canes

Weed carefully around fruit bushes and canes; then, after a spell of rain, spread a layer of organic mulch over the surface to help retain moisture and suppress the growth of weeds. Keep an eye on raspberry canes, too: they tend to be over-eager in throwing out new shoots and suckers. Pull or cut some out to avoid a dense thicket.

Protect plants against frosts

Late frosts are still a possibility in May. If you take the risk of planting tender plants outdoors, keep cloches, tunnels, fleece, or even newspapers on hand to cover them at night if the weather worsens.

HARVEST HIGHLIGHTS

Rhubarb

The stalks are ready to pick when they reach about 12in (30cm) in height. Much taller, and they'll become stringy.

Radishes

Summer radishes are fast-growing, and if you sowed or planted some seedlings outdoors last month, they may be ready now. Pull them up and eat them before they grow too large.

Turnips

The first baby turnips of the year should be ready now. Lift them while they're still young, small, and at their very best.

DON'T FORGET

- **Weed** as often as you can.
- **Thin out** seedlings ruthlessly.
- **Earth up** potatoes so the tubers growing underground are not exposed to the light.

1

2

3

4

5

1 *Clematis montana* var. *grandiflora*

30x12ft (10x4m); Zones 6–9

A vigorous climber for quick cover and attractive summer foliage. White flowers with cream anthers are produced for about four weeks in late spring and early summer.

GROW IT in sun or dappled shade against a wall, fence, or large tree, but keep the roots in shade. Plant in fertile, well-drained soil enriched with organic matter. Prune after flowering (see page 59).

2 *Paeonia daurica* subsp. *mlokosewitschii*

36x36in (90x90cm); Zones 4–9

A clump-forming herbaceous peony with lemon-yellow flowers and bluish-green leaves, ideal for a mixed border.

GROW IT in full sun or part-day shade in deep, fertile, moist but well-drained soil enriched with organic matter. Shelter from strong winds.

3 *Allium hollandicum*

3ftx4in (1mx10cm); Zones 4–9

With drumstick seedheads that look good long after the flowers fade, this bulb is the perfect highlight in a sunny, mixed border.

GROW IT in any fertile, well-drained soil, ideally in full sun, although it will tolerate light shade.

4 *Digitalis* x *mertonensis*

36x12in (90x30cm); Zones 4–9

A perennial foxglove loved by bees, with tall spires of tubular, pinkish-buff flowers in spring and early summer.

GROW IT in partial shade and humus-rich soils if possible, although it tolerates most aspects and soils if not too wet or dry.

5 *Papaver* (Oriental Group) 'Cedric Morris'

36x36in (90x90cm); Zones 3–7

A showy perennial poppy with bowl-shaped, satiny, soft-pink frilled flowers with dark centers.

GROW IT in full sun, in deep, fertile, well-drained soil. Cut back hard after flowering to produce fresh foliage and more flowers.

GET AHEAD

SOW BIENNIALS FOR NEXT YEAR'S SPRING BEDDING

Biennials are sown one year and flower the next, meaning that forward planning is key to getting the most out of them. The easiest way to remember when to sow next spring's biennial bedding plants is to do it when this year's plants are beginning to fade and are ready to be cleared away.

WHY NOT TRY?

Forget-me-nots, wallflowers, sweet Williams, winter-flowering pansies, and *Bellis perennis* can all be sown this way. They'll add a burst of color wherever you choose to plant them.

1.
Find a corner to sow the seeds (avoid reusing the same piece of ground for wallflowers, as this can lead to clubroot). Rake the soil to a fine tilth and level off.

2.
Create shallow drills about 6in (15cm) apart. Water the area if the soil is dry.

3.
Sow the seeds thinly along the row, cover lightly with dry soil, and firm gently. Label each row.

4.
In a few weeks' time, the seedlings will need to be thinned or transplanted to grow with more space between them, before being planted in their final spots in autumn.

MY GARDEN IN MAY

JUNE

Summer is well and truly here now. You won't be lacking jobs in the garden, such as cutting back and mowing, but remember to take time to enjoy the fruits of your labors. Savor the sensory delights of your garden, and reward yourself for all the hard work you have put into it.

KEY TASKS

- Continue weeding and deadheading.
- Water new and young plants as necessary.
- Finish pruning spring-flowering shrubs.
- Propagate climbers by layering them.
- Sow seeds of perennials.
- Continue to plant summer bedding plants outdoors.
- Keep fruit and vegetables well watered during dry spells.
- Shade and ventilate the greenhouse.

LAST CHANCE

Plant tomatoes now, ideally in a sunny spot. When planting tomatoes outside, leave a slight depression in the soil to help retain water around the roots of the plants when watering them.

AROUND THE GARDEN

June is the month when things hit their peak: borders look perfect, and summer vegetables and soft fruit are flourishing. Notice what has gone well and, above all, enjoy your garden — but don't forget to keep an eye on pests and be alert to drier spells, when you will need to do plenty of watering.

GENERAL CARE

Apply and renew mulches

A good idea at any time of year, mulching is crucial now because it helps reduce water loss from the soil and suppress weeds. Make sure the soil is moist beforehand, though, or it'll have the opposite effect and keep moisture out. You can also "mulch" newly planted containers. Try decorative chippings that will complement stone, terracotta, and glazed pots.

Water plants thoroughly

It's common sense to water plants during hot spells, but it's not foolproof. If you have a lot to do, it's not helpful to go out every night and splash a little water everywhere. Concentrate on newly planted plants, young vegetables, and plants in containers, as these need it most. In drought periods, divide the garden into areas and every evening give a different one a good soaking, which should last for up to a week. This is more beneficial because the roots will go deeper into the soil in search of water. Smaller amounts of water encourage the roots to come to the surface of the soil, causing more harm in the long run; roots near the surface make the plants even more vulnerable in drier conditions.

Assess gaps in borders

Before summer reaches its height, assess your borders. Any gaps are better filled with bedding plants for the summer now, then more permanent plants can be added in the autumn. These gap-fillers will give instant color to what may have been a bare patch of earth. Any annuals will do, whether hardy or half-hardy. If you need height between medium-sized plants, you can even drop in a whole pot of summer-display plants. Hardy annuals sown now will flower in late summer and autumn, extending the flowering display in the borders.

Mow the lawn as needed

Cut your lawn so that you remove only a half-inch of growth each time. This is because the less grass taken off at each cut, the healthier it will remain. It is also important to mow in a different direction each time, because if you mow in the same direction several times in a row, the grass begins to grow in that direction and the mower blades, especially those on a cylinder mower, will not cut it as well. The mower blades should be at 3in (7.5cm). If there are dry spells, reduce the frequency of mowing and irrigate regularly. Most turfgrass varieties require about an inch of water weekly during the warm season. Apply water early in the morning or late in the afternoon to minimize evaporation.

TREES, SHRUBS, AND CLIMBERS

Remove fading blooms

When rhododendron, camellia, and lilac flowers are past their best, remove them. This diverts the plant's energy from producing seeds into building up buds. Be careful when removing the spent flowers from rhododendrons and camellias, as the new shoots develop immediately below the old flowerheads and you don't want to damage this early growth. With lilacs, cut back the flowered stem to just above a pair of leaves or buds, or even small shoots, lower down the stem.

Prune mature deciduous shrubs

Keep an eye on shrubs such as deutzia, kolkwitzia, philadelphus, and weigela. Once they've finished flowering, it's time to prune them back. First, look over the whole plant and remove any dead or damaged growth, cutting to a stem joint or leaf. Then take a worm's-eye view through the thicket of stems at the base of the plant and cut out one in three quite low down, selecting the oldest and thickest for removal. Larger stems can be cut with loppers. Really tough old wood will need a pruning saw. Prune away any that occurs. After pruning, feed with a general organic fertilizer and mulch it with organic matter. The new growth produced over summer will flower next year.

Watch out for suckers on roses

June is a month for enjoying one of the most popular flowers of all: roses. To ensure these plants keep blooming for as long as possible, keep an eye out for suckers. Most modern bush roses are grafted, or budded, onto a rootstock, which gives the plant the vigor it needs to produce all those beautiful blooms. One slight drawback with budded roses, however, is that every so often the rootstock itself throws out the odd shoot—and this can divert the plant's energy from flowering. It is clearly identifiable because the foliage is generally lighter in color. It is better if suckers can be pulled off the plant at their point of origin on the roots rather than cut off. If they are cut off, the sucker is more likely to grow again. If it is pulled off, a little of the root is damaged and it is therefore less likely to be able to regrow.

" "

There is nothing better to do after a long June day than to sit in the garden with a glass of something refreshing and take in the scents, which are often stronger at this time of day.

PERENNIALS, ANNUALS, BULBS, AND BEDDING

Sow hardy herbaceous perennials outside

It's now warm enough to sow perennials like lupins, delphiniums, and hollyhocks in shallow drills in a corner of the garden. If space is limited, sow perennials in trays or small pots and place them in a cold frame or at the base of a sheltered wall. When the seedlings are large enough, repot them into individual pots and grow them during the summer. Plant them outside in the autumn.

Lift and divide bulbs

When bulbs have finished flowering and their foliage has died down, they can be lifted, dried, and stored. If you tend to leave yours in place year after year, lift overcrowded clumps now and divide them so that they can spend the summer reestablishing themselves.

Plant summer bedding plants

With the risk of a cold snap well behind us, it is safe to plant all bedding plants outdoors, including tender kinds like begonias. Look out for plants like bidens, felicia, and brachyscome as well as old favorites such as pelargoniums, salvias, and lobelia. If you haven't done so already, remove any old spring bedding, then lightly fork over the soil. Spread a little general fertilizer before planting, but not too much or the plants will produce a lot of lush growth at the expense of flowers. Water the plants well an hour or so before planting them. This is particularly important where young plants are growing together in a seed tray and the roots will be disturbed when you plant them. Don't forget to give them a thorough watering after planting, too.

TEN-MINUTE TASKS

- **Disbud** hybrid tea roses to encourage larger blooms.
- **Hoe** or hand-pull annual weeds while they are still small.
- **Continue** to stake tall-growing perennials to give them extra support in windy and rainy weather.
- **Water** all plants in containers regularly during dry spells.

CONTAINERS

Show off bedding plants in hanging baskets

Hanging baskets are surprisingly easy to plant up—and the effect far surpasses the effort. Use one of the many types of liners available from garden centers. If you use sphagnum moss, make sure it comes from a sustainable source, such as your own garden, as its excessive collection can endanger rare wildlife habitats. Use taller plants in the center to give height to the display, and tuck in plenty of trailing plants around them and around the outside of the basket. When the plants grow, the basket will be hidden and you will have a mass of flowers to enjoy all summer long. Hang your basket in a sheltered spot where you can water it easily.

Plant half-hardy annuals and tender perennials

Now that the warmer weather is here to stay—for a few months, at least—it's a good time to plant half-hardy annuals and tender perennials in tubs, troughs, and other containers outdoors. If you haven't raised any plants yourself, most garden centers will have a tempting selection of plants for sale now. Put as many plants as you can get into each container to get the best effect.

THE KITCHEN GARDEN

June signals the midpoint of the year, when we tip definitively from spring into summer. As such, it's your last chance to sow beans, carrots, and pea seeds—but it's also your first opportunity to harvest crops such as new potatoes, onions, and strawberries.

Weed out the competition

Unwanted plants crop up all around the garden (see page 58), but they can be particularly troublesome in the vegetable patch because they compete with your seedlings for moisture and nutrients. Be sure to dig out any perennial weeds, such as dandelions and creeping buttercup, that you might have overlooked in the preceding months. Then hoe regularly to prevent annual weeds from appearing. Dry, warm days are best, as the sun will dry out and kill uprooted weeds.

Summer-prune herbs

Chop back herbs such as mint, chives, sage, thyme, and lovage. By removing the tired old leaves, you'll stimulate the growth of new ones so that you can enjoy fresh herbs for that much longer. And don't let the cuttings go to waste—use them in your cooking, or dry or freeze them for use later.

Thin out apples and pears

"June drop" usually takes place toward the end of the month. Apple trees (and to a lesser extent pear trees) naturally let fall a large number of tiny, embryo fruit as a way of automatically thinning out their crop. In a good year, however, you may have to thin them out further to stop overcrowding, to allow each fruit to grow to a good size, and to avoid branches breaking under the weight of too much fruit. You'll need to do the same for plums, damsons, and peaches—once at the beginning of the month, and once again toward the end.

HARVEST HIGHLIGHTS

Strawberries

June is without doubt strawberry month. Few things signal a midsummer day more perfectly than a bowl of strawberries and cream. Check plants daily so that you can pick the berries when they are perfectly ripe and at their sweetest and juiciest.

Potatoes

Lifting the first new potatoes of the year is always a rewarding moment. Early varieties such as 'Accent', 'Annabel', 'Red Duke of York', and 'Concorde' should be ready in June—around 100–110 days after planting, depending of course on the weather and other growing factors.

Carrots

If you sowed an early variety in March or April, you should be able to pull your first carrots of the year this month. Baby carrots are wonderful in salads and need only the briefest cooking for stir-fries.

DON'T FORGET

- **Check nets:** make sure peas, cabbages and other brassicas, and soft fruit are all securely netted against birds.
- **Feed tomatoes** grown under cover with high-potash fertilizer every week as soon as they form their first tiny fruits.
- **Spread mulches,** such as garden compost, well-rotted manure, or bark chips, to suppress weeds and help retain moisture in the soil.
- **Support pole beans** by constructing rows or tripods using 8ft (2.5m) long canes and strong twine.
- **Tie in** new blackberry canes.

1 *Dianthus* 'Little Jock'

4x4in (10x10cm); Zones 4–9

The clove-scented, double, pale-pink flowers of this evergreen perennial appear just above the foliage in summer.

GROW IT in an open, sunny spot in sharply drained, gritty, slightly alkaline soil. Good drainage is essential, so on clay soils, dig in plenty of coarse sand.

2 *Geranium himalayense*

18x24in (45x60cm); Zones 4–8

In early summer, expect a profusion of white-centered, violet-blue to deep-blue flowers. Blooms continue sporadically into autumn.

GROW IT in fertile, well-drained soil in sun or partial shade. Trim after the first flush of flowers to encourage more in the autumn.

3 *Buddleja globosa*

15x15ft (5x5m); Zones 6–9

In early summer, this large shrub bursts with a profusion of honey-scented, orange-yellow flowers.

GROW IT in any fertile garden soil enriched with organic matter. A sunny spot is ideal, but it will tolerate light shade. Keep pruning to a minimum.

4 *Lupinus* 'The Page'

36x30in (90x75cm); Zones 4–8

The dense, carmine-red flower spires of this lupin are at their peak in early and mid-summer.

GROW IT in light, fertile, well-drained soil, preferably slightly acidic, in sun, though it tolerates part-day shade. Cut back after the first flush for a few more flowers late in summer.

5 *Geum* 'Borisii'

20x12in (50x30cm); Zones 4–9

Long-stemmed clusters of bright, brick-red flowers with golden-yellow stamens bloom from late spring to late summer.

GROW IT in any fertile, well-drained soil in full sun or light, part-day shade. It will thrive at the front of mixed or herbaceous borders, especially in cottage gardens.

GET AHEAD

PEG DOWN STRAWBERRY RUNNERS TO MAKE NEW PLANTS

Strawberries do not reproduce reliably from seed; instead, it's best to propagate from runners. Peg down strawberry runners in the same way you would layer a climber, and next year you'll be able to enjoy even more of these summertime favorites.

GOOD TO KNOW

You can propagate a variety of plants from runners, and not just edible ones. Try clematis, *Akebia quinata*, wisteria, and honeysuckle.

1.
Peg down a stem still attached to the plant at intervals along the ground. Roots should grow into the soil below the pegs.

2.
Either in the autumn, or next spring, carefully uproot the stem and separate each rooted section.

3.
Pot each individually in a mixture of peat-free compost and vermiculite.

4.
Water the plants thoroughly and place in a cold frame. Keep them watered over winter, then plant outside in spring.

MY GARDEN IN JUNE

JULY

In July, the garden is full of color and the scent of roses and sweet peas fills the air, especially in the long evenings. Gardening in hot weather needs to be leisurely, though it can take some energy to keep everything watered.

KEY TASKS

- Be on the alert for aphids and other pests, and get rid of them as soon as you spot them.
- Continue deadheading flowers as they fade.
- Prune shrubs that flowered in early summer and take semi-ripe cuttings from shrubs.
- Plant autumn-flowering bulbs.
- Transplant seedlings of biennials sown in May and June.
- Water vegetables regularly.
- Lift new potatoes, onions, and garlic, and pinch out pole beans at the top of their canes.
- Keep new and young plants topped off with water, and feed and water plants in containers regularly.

LAST CHANCE

If you haven't yet sown all the vegetables you plan to harvest in the autumn, now's the time to get it done. Don't forget to plant all your winter brassicas outside now, too.

AROUND THE GARDEN

July is the month for taking time to enjoy the garden, having relaxing meals al fresco, appreciating the plants, and watching the abundance of wildlife in residence. While there might still be routine work to do, this is a good month to take a slower pace.

GENERAL CARE

Use water sparingly

After a few weeks of dry weather, water is likely to be in shorter supply, so conserve as much as you can. First, mulch borders with organic matter to reduce water loss from the surface. Make sure the soil is moist before you do so. You can also collect water in a rain barrel throughout the year. In times of drought, water only the plants that really need it, such as newly planted trees and shrubs, and give them a good soaking when you do (see page 70).

Plan for vacations

July and August are generally the vacation months, and any effort you spend preparing for time away is worth it; you don't want to come back to a jungle or a sea of dead plants! Ask a neighbor, family member, or friend to water and feed plants and mow the lawn. Be sure to harvest crops like beans and zucchini in good time before you head away so they don't go to waste. If you time it right, you may even have a fresh crop ready for your return. The same goes for cutting flowers: if picked regularly, they'll produce blooms well into autumn.

Mow and trim lawn edges

To keep your lawn in good shape, mow it and trim the border edges once or twice a week. During very dry weather, raise the blades of the mower and mow less often: the grass is best left a little longer during dry periods so that the plants retain more leaf area and therefore cope better. The grass will also not be growing as vigorously, so you won't need to cut it as often. Leave clippings on the lawn to act as a mulch, helping to retain moisture in the soil. Then, when the grass gets going again in more moist conditions, the blades can be gradually lowered to their normal height again.

TREES, SHRUBS, AND CLIMBERS

Pot or plant softwood cuttings outdoors

If you took softwood cuttings earlier in the year, check whether they've rooted. As soon as they have, it's time to pot them or plant them outdoors. Be sure to water them well before and after. If you have space, line the cuttings out in a corner of the vegetable garden, where they can grow during the summer. By autumn, they'll have formed excellent plants. If you have more limited space, pot them into individual pots—but don't let them dry out.

Limit the spread of diseases

Diseases like black spot, rust, and mildew are more of a problem in summer, the first two especially if the weather has been damp. Mildew tends to appear when the weather is drier. To minimize the spread of diseases, gather up and burn all infected leaves that have fallen to the ground. Never put them on the compost heap, as this may spread the spores of the disease around the garden.

PRUNING WISTERIA

By July, wisteria's beautiful, romantic-looking blooms will be past their best. To encourage flower buds to form for next year, cut back the wispy growths made during the summer so that they are within five or six buds of the main stems.

PERENNIALS, ANNUALS, BULBS, AND BEDDING

Gather seeds from perennials

Many perennials will be finishing flowering now, and if they haven't been cut off, seed pods will be developing. A lot of seedheads will become ripe toward the end of the month and must be gathered before they open up and scatter the seeds. You will have to be vigilant if you want to catch them before they do so! Seeds are best collected on a dry, sunny day when there will be less chance of rot getting into them. Put the seeds into paper envelopes, seal, and label them. Store them somewhere cool and dry.

Give annuals and tender perennials a pick-me-up

To keep the display going well into the autumn, you'll need to show annuals and tender perennials a bit of love in July. Deadhead old flowers regularly to prevent the plants from setting seed (unless, of course, you want to collect seeds from some plants). Plants such as pansies and petunias tend to get straggly now, and picking off individual spent flowers from these plants can be tedious. An easy way to deadhead them is to cut them back with pruners or shears. Cut them back quite hard, give them a quick tonic with a high-potash fertilizer, and new growth will soon be produced with flowers later in the summer.

DIVIDING IRISES

After several years, bearded and other rhizomatous irises tend to lose vigor, so once they've flowered, they'll need to be divided. Lift the clump carefully with a fork, then cut off the younger pieces with a sharp knife, discarding the older pieces. Cut off faded leaves, and cut across the remaining foliage about 6in (15cm) from the root, leaving a fan shape of trimmed leaves. Replant in groups in a sunny spot, 3–6in (8–15cm) apart, the rhizome just below the surface. Water them thoroughly.

CONTAINERS

Spruce up containers

To extend the colorful displays of your containers well into autumn, you'll need to water and feed them regularly—potentially even twice a day during very hot spells. Don't be fooled by rain, either: containers will still need plenty of water in wet weather as the mass of roots inside the container and the foliage on top make rain penetration almost impossible. Deadhead the plants regularly to keep the plants looking good and prevent them from setting seed. Plants crammed together in containers can sometimes start to look a little straggly toward the end of the summer, so go over your containers occasionally, pruning off any straggly shoots and any that are crowding out other plants. You can always make some cuttings from the material you cut off.

Plant autumn-flowering bulbs

To guarantee a bit of color after summer has faded, plant autumn-flowering bulbs in containers now. You'll get flowers all through September, October, and—if the weather is reasonable—even into November. The flowers will appear without foliage because the leaves will have died down during the summer; the leaves will follow in the spring.

TEN-MINUTE TASKS

- **Assess** your borders while they are in full bloom, and note down any adjustments to make later in the year.
- **Remove** any unwanted growth from the bases or trunks of trees and shrubs.
- **Continue** to water plants if the weather is dry.
- **Spot-treat** any perennial weeds that appear among alpines.

THE KITCHEN GARDEN

July is a month of plenty: with a bit of luck, you'll be harvesting something delicious from your plot almost every day. But hotter temperatures can also mean less rain — so be sure to keep on top of watering.

Water to prevent bolting

Certain vegetables, such as lettuces, arugula, spinach, and cauliflowers, have a natural tendency to flower and go to seed as days lengthen and temperatures rise. Regular watering can delay or even prevent bolting.

Pinch out pole beans and tomato shoots

Pole beans don't really know when to stop. Pinch out the growing tips when they reach the top of your canes or they will quickly become tangled and top-heavy. For tomatoes, nip out the side shoots that appear in the "V" between leaf stems and the main stems of vine tomatoes. And pinch out the growing tip at the top of the plant once four or five trusses have formed — unless you have plenty of support for the plant to ramble upon.

Feed tomatoes and peppers

As soon as you see that the first fruits have formed, it's time to start watering tomatoes and peppers regularly with a liquid feed. Feeding encourages both flowers and fruits.

Earth up brassicas and potatoes

Pull earth up around the stalks of Brussels sprouts and other brassicas if they seem unsteady, and give them a top-dressing of nitrogenous fertilizer or an organic liquid feed. Keep an eye on potatoes and, if necessary, continue to earth them up.

HARVEST HIGHLIGHTS

Green beans

The first green beans of the year are certainly the best. Don't hold back and leave them too long or they'll turn stringy.

Zucchini

July is the start of the season for zucchini. They are capable of doubling in size in a single day, so inspect regularly and harvest often.

Tomatoes

In warmer areas of the country, this will be your first month for tomatoes. Resist temptation and leave them on the vine until they are as ripe, sweet, and juicy as possible.

Peas

The first peas of the year are always the sweetest and tastiest. Pick them while they're still young and, if you can, eat them immediately.

DON'T FORGET

- **Inspect** tomatoes and potatoes for any signs of blight, such as withering leaves or browning fruits.
- **Check** all wire-trained trees to ensure that ties are secure but not too tight. Tie in or summer-prune new growth.
- **Cover** heads of cauliflowers by pulling outside leaves over them and tying them in place to stop the white heads from turning yellow in the sun.
- **Secure nets** around peas, brassicas, and soft fruits to keep off scavenging birds.
- **Dry out** garlic, onions, and shallots by lifting the bulbs and leaving them in the sun. The more thoroughly you dry them, the longer they will keep.

1 *Rosa* 'Chinatown'

4x3ft (1.2x1m); Zones 5–9

From summer to autumn, these modern shrub roses bear beautifully scented double, deep-yellow blooms.

GROW IT in sun in deep, fertile, moist but well-drained soil, as you would bush roses. They're ideal in shrub and mixed borders, as hedges, or as specimen plants.

2 *Nigella damascena* 'Miss Jekyll'

20x9in (50x23cm); Zones 2–11

During summer, this plant produces sky-blue flowers, surrounded by a ruff of slender leaves, likely inspiring its common name: love-in-a-mist.

GROW IT in full sun in any moderately fertile, well-drained soil. It works well in annual borders, cutting borders, or cottage gardens. Protect with cloches in very cold, wet winters.

3 *Helianthus annuus* 'Teddy Bear'

3ftx12in (90x30cm); Zones 2–11

This double sunflower with fluffy, golden-yellow blooms is a summer showstopper.

GROW IT in full sun in fertile, well-drained soil in a warm, sheltered site. Sow seeds under glass in small pots in early spring, or in the flowering site in late spring.

4 *Hebe* 'Gauntlettii'

3x3ft (1x1m); Zones 9–10

This neat, bushy evergreen shrub bears hanging clusters of small pink flowers from late summer until late autumn.

GROW IT in fertile, well-drained, neutral to alkaline soil in sun or dappled shade. Shelter from cold winds.

5 *Lobelia erinus* Waterfall Series

10x12in (26x30cm); Zones 2–11

From midsummer to late autumn, this lobelia plant is covered in small, star-shaped blue or white flowers.

GROW IT in borders of containers in a sunny spot. Sow indoors in spring, then transplant into pots and grow indoors until the threat of frost has passed.

GET AHEAD

FILL YOUR BORDERS WITH FREE SHRUBS

For an easy and cost-effective way to increase your stock of shrubs, take semi-ripe cuttings from growth made this year once the stems have started to turn woody at the base. The cuttings will root in about six to eight weeks, when they can be potted and grown. They'll be a decent size in a few years.

WHY NOT TRY?

Semi-ripe cuttings from evergreen shrubs work particularly well. Try *Camellia*, *Mahonia*, *Berberis*, and *Ceanothus*.

1.

Remove shoots about 4in (10cm) long with a sliver or heel of older bark from the main stem, or trim below a leaf joint.

2.

Trim the tail of the heel off, if there is one, then remove the lower leaves. If growth is very soft, pinch out the tip.

3.

Wearing protective gloves, dip the whole cutting in a fungicide solution. Then dip the base in hormone rooting solution.

4.

Put the cuttings around the edge of a pot containing peat-free seed-starting mix and water well.

5.

Put a plastic bag over the pot to create a humid atmosphere, and put the pot in a shady part of the garden.

MY GARDEN IN JULY

....
....
....
....
....
....
....
....
....
....
....
....
....
....
....
....
....
....
....
....

AUGUST

August is sure to bring hot, sultry days, so keep everything well-watered and make preparations if you're going on vacation. When you're at home, take time to enjoy your garden, but be sure to check off a few jobs from the list so that it thrives well into autumn.

KEY TASKS

- Feed and water all plants that need it regularly.
- Deadhead flowers as they fade, and prune rambling roses after flowering.
- Trim hedges back into shape.
- Take cuttings from tender perennials.
- Collect ripening seed from plants you wish to keep.
- Prop up heavily laden fruit tree branches, and summer-prune gooseberry and red currant plants.
- Harvest the first apples and pears. Keep tomatoes and peppers picked.

LAST CHANCE

As the height of summer is now behind us, this is your last opportunity to summer-prune apple, pear, and other trained fruit trees before they begin to produce fruit.

AROUND THE GARDEN

On the hottest days, put down your tools and simply enjoy your garden. The refreshing cool of the evening is much more pleasant to work in, and light summer maintenance is all it takes to keep the garden looking its very best.

GENERAL CARE

Look out for self-sown seedlings

In August, you'll still need to weed borders regularly, but keep an eye out for any self-sown seedlings from your own plants. It is surprising what you can find. Most hybrids and many cultivars of plants will not reproduce true from seed, but the seedlings that do emerge can throw up all sorts of variations in flower color, plant growth habit, and even leaf color. You never know when you might discover a winner of a plant in your own backyard.

Protect plants from slugs

In damp summers, slug damage can be rather dispiriting. Unfortunately, the lusher and greener foliage is, the more they like it! Birds, ground beetles, and frogs all eat slugs, so the more they can be encouraged into the garden the better. Put down pieces of slate or wood in the border for slugs to creep under. They like dark, cool, moist hiding places. These traps can then be turned over, exposing the slugs to any birds in the vicinity—or you can pick them up and dispose of them yourself. Besides the popular beer traps (see page 32), you can also try placing inverted hollow grapefruit or orange halves around the border. Hollowed-out potatoes also work as decoys if you're trying to protect a potato crop. Plants that are particularly prone to slug attack can be surrounded with a layer of crushed eggshells or gravel: slugs don't like the coarse surface and so are less likely to reach the plants.

Switch up your lawn feed

By late summer, avoid high-nitrogen fertilizers for lawns; they promote vigorous growth, which will not stand up to the rigors of the winter. Instead, choose fertilizers high in phosphates, as these promote root growth, toughening up the grass for the winter ahead. Apply all fertilizers according to the manufacturer's instructions, and make sure you do so when it is going to rain, as the fertilizer needs to soak in. A wheeled fertilizer spreader will take the guesswork out of applying the feed and saves the chore of marking out the area to do it by hand. You may be able to rent one from your local garden center.

TREES, SHRUBS, AND CLIMBERS

Trim hedges

By this point in the year, most hedges will have finished growing, so the end of August is a good time to give them their final trim. The only exception to this is conifers, as they may need another going-over. If you want a level top to your hedge, put a dowel in the ground at either end and tie twine between them at the required height. The process is the same whether you're using a powered hedge trimmer or hand shears. First, trim the sides of the hedge, working from the bottom up. The reason for working upward is that as you cut, the trimmings will fall away and you will be better able to see where you are going. Make the hedge wider at the base and narrower at the top to help it stand up to the weather. The top can be trimmed last, using the twine as a guide.

GIVING LAVENDER A TRIM

Lavender's fragrant, blue-purple flowers are at their best now. To keep the plants bushy and compact, you'll want to remove the old flower spikes. Go over the plants with a pair of hand shears, cutting off the old flower spikes and about 1 in (2.5cm) of the leafy growth at the tips of the shoots. This will encourage new side shoots to grow.

PERENNIALS, ANNUALS, BULBS, AND BEDDING

Keep chrysanthemums and dahlias looking their best

Chrysanthemum and dahlia blooms look terrific all the way from late summer to the first frosts. But they both have one problem: the flowers are irresistible to earwigs, which eat the blooms. The best way to control these insects is to put upturned pots filled with straw or shredded newspaper on the top of canes among the plants. Earwigs love to crawl into dark places during the day, so they'll find their way into the pots instead of your blooms. In the morning you can empty the pots of earwigs far away from your flowers. Earwigs aren't always pests, though: they can be very helpful for reducing aphids on fruit trees and shrubs.

Cut back overgrown perennials

Summer isn't all sun, of course. In wet weather a lot of taller-growing perennials, especially achilleas, tend to flop over and smother other, smaller neighbors. Trim them back to give smaller plants a chance to recover and flower. The cut-back plants may also grow again and produce some flowers in the autumn. You may find that perennials have spread over the lawn, too. If so, trim them back and assess the damage. If the grass underneath has been killed off, give it a good watering and a dose of lawn fertilizer and it will very quickly regrow.

TEN-MINUTE TASKS

- **Cut back** hardy geraniums to make them look neater and to encourage new growth. You may even get flowers later in autumn.
- **Weed** between alpines and top them off with fresh gravel: it looks nice, keeps weeds down, and helps retain moisture in the soil.
- **Deadhead** roses. Removing the fading flowers prevents plants from putting energy into producing seeds—so you may get new flowers.
- **Plan ahead** for vacations. Make sure you have enlisted someone to look after your precious garden if you're planning a getaway (see page 84).

Take cuttings from geraniums and fuchsias

August is the traditional month for taking cuttings from tender perennials. Though they can be taken any time from spring through autumn, now is your last chance until spring to pot them. The cuttings are very easy to take, and only those of geraniums differ in one or two ways. All cuttings should be removed from the parent plant by cutting off strong, nonflowering shoots just above a bud, leaving a cutting about 4in (10cm) long. Trim the lower leaves off and then trim the cutting immediately below a leaf joint. With all geraniums, remove the stipules — the little papery flaps — at the base of the leaf stalks. Geraniums root perfectly well without hormone rooting solution, but all other perennials will benefit from it. Insert the cuttings around the edge of small pots containing seed-starting mix (half peat-free medium, half perlite or vermiculite), and place all kinds except geraniums in a lidded propagator (the fine hairs on the leaves will trap moisture and may cause the cuttings to rot). Place the pots either on a windowsill or in a shady part of the greenhouse. The cuttings will root in about four weeks, when you can repot them to overwinter under cover.

CONTAINERS

Feed permanent plants in containers

Shrubs, perennials, and trees in containers need looking after just as much as temporary summer bedding plants. Water and feed them regularly, and—especially with woody plants—use a high-potash fertilizer to encourage the wood to ripen rather than soft, sappy growth, which may become damaged in winter.

Make watering easy

In truly hot spells, it pays to be both practical and prudent. Group all your containers together in a shady spot, if this is possible. Not only does this make things quicker when it comes to watering, but it also benefits the plants: a more humid atmosphere is maintained around the leaves where plants are clustered together. This isn't usually recommended, as crowded growth encourages diseases to spread, but it's fine for a week or two during peaks of hot weather. You can also take hanging baskets down and group them with the others by perching them on buckets or on upturned pots.

Pot herbs for winter

No store-bought herb can compete with a homegrown one. To keep your supply of herbs such as chives going through winter, now is a good time to pot them. Lift a clump of chives from the garden; if it is fairly large, split it into smaller clumps. This way you may get several pieces to pot. Put each piece into a pot with peat-free commercial potting mix, cut back the old foliage, and water them. Set the pots on a windowsill or in a cool greenhouse or conservatory. In a few weeks you will have a fresh supply of chives.

" "

It might be hard to believe, but plant growth really starts to slow down from the end of August—so don't forget to put down your tools once in a while and drink it all in before autumn.

THE KITCHEN GARDEN

August is often a month of plenty, as many of the plants you've nurtured through the spring and early summer will be coming to fruition now. This may leave you with one problem, though—what to do with any surplus!

Harvest regularly

You'll be—quite literally—reaping the rewards of your hard work in many areas of the kitchen garden this month, and you don't want to miss any produce when it's at its best. Keep an especially close eye on zucchini, pole beans, and green beans as they grow notoriously quickly at this time of year. Check them every day and harvest regularly, making sure you pick them before they grow too large and become stringy.

Prop up heavily laden fruit trees

In particularly good years, apples, pears, peaches, and plums can bow so severely with the weight of their fruit that the branches are in danger of breaking before it is ready to be harvested. Support the branches—especially young or weak ones—with rope ties or props to keep them from cracking.

Feed pumpkins and winter squashes

With autumn now on the horizon, it's time to turn your attention to these Halloween favorites. For monster growth, feed pumpkins and winter squashes once a week with high-potash tomato fertilizer. In damp weather, lift them off the soil onto bricks or planks of wood or they may rot.

Earth up brassicas, potatoes, and celery

Keep earthing up potatoes, trench celery, and brassicas by drawing up soil around the plants. Potato tubers must remain underground or they will turn green and may become poisonous, while celery stems are tender only when blanched—that is, kept out of the light. Finally, earthing up brassicas gives the stems extra support.

HARVEST HIGHLIGHTS

Peaches and nectarines

Both peaches and nectarines will be ripening this month. Pick the fruits when they're slightly soft and pull away easily.

Eggplants

In the heat of August, eggplants will be fattening up—as long as you're able to give them the water they need. Harvest them when they are at their blackest and glossiest.

Chiles and peppers

Most peppers become sweeter as they ripen, and most chiles become hotter. Yet the rule barely applies to the innocent-looking, peach-colored 'Habanero'; this chile is blisteringly hot, whatever stage you pick it.

DON'T FORGET

- **Pick** early apples and pears. Twist, rather than pull, the fruit; if they come away easily, they're ready to enjoy.
- **Check** sweet corn for smut (a fungus), and remove any affected cobs.
- **Spread** any leftover rotted-down compost as mulch before starting a new compost heap.
- **Protect** carrot crops from carrot flies with fleece or physical barriers.

1 *Dierama pulcherrimum*

5ftx24in (1.5mx60cm); Zones 7–10

A graceful perennial with wandlike flower spires, the so-called angel's fishing rod produces bell-shaped, pale to deep magenta-pink flowers in summer.

GROW IT in full sun in leafy, fertile, well-drained soil. Keep well watered in dry weather.

2 *Crocosmia* x *crocosmiiflora* 'Jackanapes'

24x3in (60x8cm); Zones 6–9

This perennial's striking sprays of orange-red and yellow flowers arch up out of sword-shaped leaves in late summer.

GROW IT in fertile soil in mixed or herbaceous borders, in full sun or partial shade. On heavy clay, plant on a layer of coarse gravel.

3 *Solenostemon scutellarioides* 'Winsome'

1½x3ft (0.5x1m); Zones 2–11

This bushy annual has vibrant, velvety leaves.

GROW IT in humus-rich, moist but well-drained soil in a sheltered spot. It works well in containers and borders.

4 *Hydrangea paniculata* 'Grandiflora'

22x8ft (7x2.5m); Zones 3–7

In late summer and early autumn, this hydrangea produces large, conical heads of white flowers that flush pink with age and are great for drying.

GROW IT in partial shade or sun in fertile, moisture-retentive, humus-rich soil. It best suits a shrub or mixed border or a woodland garden.

5 *Phygelius* x *rectus* 'Salmon Leap'

4x5ft (1.2x1.5m); Zones 7–10

Throughout summer and into autumn, this evergreen shrub produces tubular orange flowers that hang from slender stalks.

GROW IT in sun in fertile, moist but well-drained soil, ideally in a shrub or mixed border or against a sunny wall.

GET AHEAD

POT PREPARED BULBS FOR CHRISTMAS FLOWERS

On hot and humid August days, winter festivities might feel a world away—but forcing bulbs now will guarantee you a welcome burst of color and fragrance by the time Christmas comes around.

WHY NOT TRY?

Bulbs to force for Christmas include amaryllis, hyacinths, and 'Paper White' narcissi.

1.

Plant several bulbs in a bowl or pot, close enough together so they are almost touching.

2.

Cover them with potting mix, leaving just the nose of the bulbs uncovered. If you are planting them in bulb bowls that have no drainage holes, use bulb fiber; otherwise, any proprietary potting compost will do.

3.

Next "plunge" the containers outside by burying them in the ground, leaving the rim of the pot above the surface. Then cover them with potting mix. Alternatively, put them in a cool, dark place indoors.

4.

After six to eight weeks, start inspecting the bulbs every day. When they have made about 1in (2.5cm) of growth, they can be brought inside, where they should be kept in cool conditions.

....
....
....
....
....
....
....
....
....
....
....
....
....
....
....
....
....
....
....

SEPTEMBER

September can often be a wonderful month in the garden. The sultry heat of high summer has gone, and the air feels fresher. You'll be gathering in the harvest and watching rich autumn colors develop—a hint of the glorious shades to come.

KEY TASKS

- Start clearing autumn debris to prevent pests and diseases from overwintering.
- Remove fallen leaves from ponds to avoid a buildup of nutrients in the water.
- Sow or sod new lawns, and dethatch and aerate more established ones.
- Begin dividing overgrown perennials.
- Plant some spring-flowering bulbs (but not tulips), plant spring-flowering biennials, and plant containers with spring bedding.
- Lift tender perennials and bring them under cover.
- Continue to harvest apples and pears.

LAST CHANCE

The weather might still be on the warm side, but if your festive plans include flowering amaryllis, hyacinths, and narcissi, now's your last chance to force the bulbs (see page 106).

AROUND THE GARDEN

By the end of September, there's a distinct chill in the morning air — and after the slight lull in garden activity over summer, there suddenly seems to be a lot to be getting on with.

GENERAL CARE

Assess your garden

Now that the summer growing season has ended, it's a good time to wander around your garden, assessing how plants have performed and whether you should move or even remove them. Write it all down so that you have something to come back to in the darker months when the colors of summer are difficult to remember. Sometimes you will have to be tough: if a plant hasn't lived up to expectations, it has to go. You don't want to spend time and money on a plant that won't grow well whatever you try. Take a step back, too, and think about how plants have been combined: did they look good together? Jot down any plants you'd like to move, so that you're ready to go when the weather conditions allow (see page 146).

Cultivate clay soil

Just as the best-laid plans start with solid foundations, the best gardens start with good soil. If your soil is particularly heavy and claylike, you may find it difficult to cultivate, especially if it hasn't been worked for several years. Now is a good time to dig it, as the soil should be fairly dry. This will give the winter weather plenty of time to help break down lumps of soil, ready for making seedbeds or for planting in spring. Roughly dig the soil, incorporating plenty of organic matter, and leave it rough for the winter. To permanently improve the drainage, dig in pea gravel. Combined with the organic matter, this will also raise the level of the soil slightly, so it will drain more easily and warm up faster in spring.

Dethatch and aerate your lawn

Over time, a layer of dead grass and debris, or "thatch," accumulates in any lawn. If left, it can restrict air movement and affect surface drainage, encouraging moss and other weeds. From late August through fall, remove it by either raking it out with a spring-tined rake or using a dethatching mower blade. Be warned: the lawn will look messy after dethatching, but it will do it a world of good and it will soon recover.

The next job is aeration. Like any plant, grass needs air and the surface of the lawn gets very compacted over the summer, with constant use and weekly cutting. To relieve this, aerate the lawn by pushing a fork into the ground to a depth of 6in (15cm) at 6–7in (15–18cm) intervals (or use an aerator). Top-dress immediately after aerating to ensure the holes stay open. A mix of three parts sieved garden soil, two parts coarse sand, and one part sieved garden compost (or old potting mix, if you have some) is the best top-dressing to use.

TREES, SHRUBS, AND CLIMBERS

Plant container-grown trees and shrubs

Autumn is a good time to plant trees and shrubs grown in containers: the soil is still quite warm and moist, so the roots can establish before winter sets in and the plants will get off to a flying start in spring. This also means you don't need to pay so much attention to watering. Plant them as you would container-grown perennials, but stake trees. Hold off planting bare-root plants of deciduous trees and shrubs until November.

Take hardwood rose cuttings

Roses are normally propagated by budding: grafting a bud of the chosen variety onto a rootstock. This is easy and quick, but it has a downside. The rootstock often throws up suckers, which can take over the whole bush. To avoid this issue, take hardwood cuttings. Select a shoot about as thick as a pencil and 12in (30cm) long. Remove the soft growing tip and all but the top three sets of leaves. Trim the base of the cutting just below a leaf joint, making the cutting about 9in (23cm) long. Make a slit trench in the ground and, if your soil is heavy clay, put some coarse sand in the bottom to assist the drainage process. Set cuttings along the trench to two-thirds of their length and firm in. The cuttings will take root ready to transplant to their flowering positions next autumn.

PERENNIALS, ANNUALS, BULBS, AND BEDDING

Choose new perennials

Make the most of autumn's moist but still-warm soil to plant new perennials. Garden centers should have a good selection of flowering and foliage herbaceous perennials, so now is a great time to enjoy deciding what plants to buy. Perennials are generally not expensive—and, of course, many plants can be lifted and divided and cuttings taken in years to come, so each plant then costs almost nothing.

While this is all very exciting, try not to get carried away: make sure the plants you choose are right for your garden and for the position they are intended for. It's a waste of money to buy something just because it is appealing, only to find it struggles or even dies because it was a bad choice. Look for plants with strong, healthy growth; the root balls should be showing plenty of roots, but not so packed that the plants are pot-bound. Water the plants well before and after planting. If they seem rather dry when you buy them, plunge them in a bucket of water to ensure the root ball is fully moist.

Plant spring-flowering biennials

Now's the time to plant spring-flowering biennials you've been growing in nursery rows through the summer (see page 66). Clear the old summer bedding away when the flowers have died off. Incorporate organic matter into the soil, then rake it level and mark out informal drifts with a stick. Remember not to grow wallflowers in the same ground as last year to avoid clubroot. Make sure the crown of each plant is level with the soil, and firm them in well. Water plants to settle the soil around the roots.

Naturalize bulbs in grass

September is the main month for planting spring-flowering bulbs, but it's still too early for tulips. Consider chionodoxa, puschkinia, ornithogalum, scilla, and *Iris histrioides*. Grape hyacinths are essentials, too.

Bulbs look spectacular when they are naturalized in grass. You can do this with all bulbs, except the tiniest alpines. The easiest way to plant smaller bulbs or corms like miniature daffodils is to lift a piece of sod and place the bulbs in groups on the soil, replacing the sod afterwards. With larger bulbs, use a bulb planter. The general rule is to plant them two to three times their own depth and add fertilizer.

CONTAINERS

Clear out summer bedding plants

Once summer bedding plants in containers have finished, clear them out and replace with spring bedding plants. Remove some of the old potting mix and add fresh. Plants and color schemes are entirely up to you, so let your imagination run wild. If you haven't raised your own spring bedding, like wallflowers, forget-me-nots, and bellis, garden centers will have a wide range to choose from. Remember to plant bulbs in with the spring bedding too.

Plant bulbs in containers

Prepare a stunning show for next spring by planting bulbs now: one kind or color of bulb for each container guarantees visual impact. Pack them in closely. There is no need to renew the potting mix when summer bedding has been pulled out, as bulbs will thrive well in the old mix. The most important time to feed bulbs is after they have flowered, when they are building up to flower again the following year.

Give permanent plants one last feed

In September, plants like shrubs, trees, and fruit trees growing in containers will need one last feed with sulphate of potash or rock potash. This will help ripen the wood, making it more able to stand up to the rigors of winter. After this, stop feeding them with general fertilizers—if fed, they'll produce soft growth, which may be damaged in the colder months.

TEN-MINUTE TASKS

- **Repair** small bare patches on the lawn by sowing seed.
- **Move** pots of tender perennials, such as fuchsias and geraniums, under cover for the winter.
- **Clear** debris in borders and remove yellowing leaves on plants to avoid the spread of diseases and pests.

THE KITCHEN GARDEN

By September, your early crops will be coming to an end—if they haven't already done so—which means it's time for later crops to have their time in the spotlight. This month, you'll harvest late potatoes and winter squashes, and you might even have your first Brussels sprouts.

Turn your compost heap

As autumn closes in, it might feel somewhat gloomy to see so many plants dying—but how satisfying to know that their goodness won't be wasted. As you add this autumn's mass of dead plant material to your heap, turn it regularly with a fork to aerate it and stimulate decomposition. Water it if it's dry, and cover to keep it warm.

Collect and save seeds

It's well worth saving certain seeds for sowing next year—especially plants you're fond of and that may be hard to find commercially. Bean, pea, squash, pumpkin, melon, and tomato seeds can all be saved, dried, stored, and sown again—although not F1 hybrid varieties, which don't come true the following year.

Sow green manures

September is a good time to sow alfalfa, annual ryegrass, and phacelia as so-called green manures—that is, plants grown specifically to be dug back into the soil. These crops will overwinter and can be dug into the ground next spring to improve the structure of the soil, release nutrients, and to act as a protective covering, smothering weeds and sheltering soil from the leaching or compacting effects of heavy rain.

HARVEST HIGHLIGHTS

Apples

There's no shortage of apples to pick this month—both the last of the early varieties and the first of the mid or late varieties. Fruit that is ripe and ready to pick should come away with a gentle twist of the hand, and with its stalk still attached.

Onions

Lift any remaining onions this month. Dry them out and hang them up somewhere cool and well ventilated. They should last for several months.

Winter squashes

Begin harvesting pumpkins and winter squashes such as the small, nutty 'Uchiki Kuri'. They will keep for longer if you dry or "cure" them in the sun to harden their skins.

DON'T FORGET

- **Water** when necessary: if rainfall is scarce and temperatures remain high, continue to water all crops regularly.
- **Cut down** tall, feathery asparagus foliage to just 1in (2.5cm) above the ground.
- **Pick** all remaining green tomatoes by the first hard freeze (around the end of the month) and ripen them indoors.
- **Stake** Brussels sprouts if they become top-heavy, or earth up the stems.
- **Order** new fruit trees and bushes now for the widest choice before planting next month.

1

2

3

4

5

1 *Stipa gigantea*

8x4ft (2.5x1.2m); Zones 5–10

In summer, tall, arching stems bear open flowerheads of silvery, purple-green spikelets that turn gold as they ripen.

GROW IT in any moderately fertile soil in full sun, although it tolerates light shade and heavy clay soils. It makes a good addition to a border.

2 *Viburnum opulus* 'Compactum'

5x5ft (1.5x1.5m); Zones 3–8

A slow-growing but sturdy shrub, this plant produces glossy, bright-red fruits in autumn.

GROW IT in any reasonably fertile, well-drained soil in sun or dappled shade. It works well in shrub borders, woodland gardens, or informal hedging.

3 *Dahlia* 'Bishop of Llandaff'

$3\frac{1}{2}$ftx18in (1.1mx45cm); Zones 3–11

From late summer until late autumn, this tender perennial produces peony-like, semi-double velvety, glowing-red flowers.

GROW IT in full sun in fertile, well-drained soil enriched with well-rotted organic matter.

4 *Agapanthus* 'Blue Giant'

4x2ft (1.2mx60cm); Zones 8–10

From midsummer through the warm days of September, this plant displays striking rich-blue flowers clustered into large spheres.

GROW IT in moist but well-drained soil. It thrives in full sun but will tolerate light, dappled shade.

5 *Clematis viticella*

12x5ft (4x1.5m); Zones 4–11

This late-flowering species is slender but tough, bearing blue to purple and red blooms.

GROW IT in fertile, well-drained soil enriched with well-rotted organic matter. For the best flowers, give the top-growth sun but keep the roots shaded with stone slabs or nearby plants.

GET AHEAD

SOW HARDY ANNUALS FOR FLOWERING NEXT YEAR

Surely all gardeners cherish the knowledge that dull-looking earth is incubating a riot of color. Now is a good month to start the process: sown now, some hardy annuals will flower from early May the following year.

WHY NOT TRY?

Next year's warmer months might feel distant, but these blooms will be worth the wait. Choose from the likes of *Calendula officinalis*, *Centaurea cyanus*, *Papaver somniferum*, California poppies (*Eschscholzia*), and *Limnanthes douglasii*.

1.

Rake the soil to a fine tilth and mark out informal areas with a stick or sand poured out of an empty wine bottle.

2.

Take out shallow drills within each marked area and water them if the soil is dry.

3.

Sow the seeds thinly, then cover them with dry soil.

4.

When the seedlings have grown to approximately 1in (2.5cm), thin them out to about 4in (10cm). In spring, you may have to thin them out again.

5.

If your soil is heavy clay, seedlings may rot. In this case, sow the seeds in cell trays and overwinter them in a cold frame, planting them outside in the spring.

MY GARDEN IN SEPTEMBER

OCTOBER

Fall tree colors are at their best this month, with only a short time to appreciate them before the leaves finish falling. If you have planted your garden with fall and winter in mind, expect company: garden birds will be attracted to the bright fruits and berries on your trees and shrubs.

KEY TASKS

- Rake up fallen leaves and make leaf mold.
- Collect berries from trees and shrubs for sowing.
- Plant climbers, perennials, and spring-blooming bulbs.
- Cut down the dying tops of perennial vegetables.
- Divide any overgrown perennials.
- Attach grease bands to apple and pear tree trunks to stop winter moths from laying eggs.
- Insulate the greenhouse and make sure the heaters work.

LAST CHANCE

Any apples and pears that haven't already been enjoyed (by wildlife or humans) need to be harvested now, before they get damaged.

AROUND THE GARDEN

The nights are drawing in and temperatures are dropping, but the garden still has much to keep us occupied—from planting trees and shrubs to collecting and storing seeds.

GENERAL CARE

Rake up fallen leaves

Why is it that every time the lawn is cleared, another gust of wind causes yet more leaves to fall? Disheartening as it might be, take comfort in the fact that this season doesn't last long—and the effort is well worth it. If leaves are left in a thick layer on the lawn, they will kill the grass. Don't forget to clear fallen leaves from borders too, or you risk encouraging slugs and snails.

Make leaf mold

Autumn leaves piled up and left to rot for a year or two will make the most wonderful organic matter to use as a mulch or a soil conditioner, called leaf mold. Leaves can, of course, be mixed with other material and put on the compost heap, but if you want leaf mold, they will need a heap of their own. A simple container will suffice:

hammer four stakes into the ground to make a square and nail chicken wire around them. The netting helps keep the leaves in one place. After about eighteen months to two years you should have good, crumbly leaf mold. Use it as a mulch or dig it into the soil as you would garden compost.

Prepare empty areas of soil

Dig over bare soil that you plan to sow later. This might not be the most exciting garden task, but now is a better time than most to check it off your list: the soil should be moist but not too sticky, and the weather tends not to be too warm or cold—ideal for exercise. Sow green manure crops (see page 114) to cover and condition soil that will otherwise be bare over winter. Green manures that will stand through winter, to be dug in in spring, include annual rye, buckwheat, and alfalfa.

TREES, SHRUBS, AND CLIMBERS

Take preventative measures

There's no escaping the fact that harsher weather is on the horizon, and time spent preparing now will save your plants—and a few headaches—later down the line. Tall shrubs such as lavateras and *Buddleja davidii*, which will be pruned hard in the spring, can be cut back now by about half their height to prevent wind rock. If plants have a lot of top growth, they can catch the wind and be blown around. When this happens, a hole forms in the soil at the base of the stem, where water collects, causing the stem to rot. In cold weather the water can freeze, causing even more damage. Check all newly planted trees, shrubs, and hedging plants. If they are loose, firm them in again carefully, adding a stake if needed.

Collect berries for sowing

Besides clearing leaves, there can hardly be a more autumnal activity than collecting berries from trees and shrubs for sowing. You can grow cotoneasters, *Rosa rugosa*, gaultheria, and all sorbus from berries. Berries don't generally need warm conditions to germinate; quite the contrary, most need to go through a period of cold to break the seed dormancy. This is called "stratification." First remove the berries, then separate the seeds, dry them off, and store them in a cool place. Sow the seeds in trays or small pots of potting mix, covering the seeds with sand. Place the container outside in a cold frame, or in a sheltered place covered with a sheet of glass to keep excessive rain out. Alternatively, stratify the seeds artificially. Mix the seed with moistened vermiculite or coarse sand in a plastic bag and place it in a refrigerator for about six weeks. Check them regularly and, when they start to germinate, take them out and sow in trays or pots.

Plant hardy container-grown climbers

As long as your climbers are hardy enough to survive their first winter when young, now's a good time to plant them outside. As you would for container-grown trees and shrubs, dig a deep hole and work some organic matter into the bottom—leaf mold and a sprinkle of bone meal is ideal because it conditions the soil without adding too much nitrogen. Then tie them into their support. The surface of the plant's root ball should be level with the soil's surface.

PERENNIALS, ANNUALS, BULBS, AND BEDDING

Check any bulbs being forced

If any top growth is being made, bring bulbs that are being forced into the light in a cool place (see page 106). Before you do, knock them out of their containers to see the root system. If there aren't many roots, put them back in the dark for a few more weeks.

Protect alpines from wet conditions

This is the time of year when alpines will appreciate protection from the wet weather. It's not the cold that alpine plants mind, but the damp. This is why some are grown in alpine houses, where there is no heat in the winter and plenty of ventilation. Proper alpine houses have extra ventilators to keep a good through-flow of air at all times, but an ordinary unheated greenhouse, or even a cold frame, will make a perfectly good home for alpines. Of course, not all alpines have to be grown in an alpine house, and those growing outside can be protected from the rain quite easily by using a cloche, with the ends left open for ventilation, or a piece of glass or rigid clear plastic supported on bricks. Weight the sheet down with extra bricks to prevent it from being lifted off by winds. If you have a raised alpine bed, then with a little improvisation you can make a mini-greenhouse with open sides to protect the plants through the winter.

Lifting dahlia tubers

All the care you put into lifting and storing dahlia tubers now will prove its worth in summer when these colorful blooms are at their most striking. First, cut the plants from their supports and trim the stems back to about 4in (10cm) from ground level. Then use a garden fork to dig carefully around the plant so as not to damage the tubers underground. Shake off as much of the old soil as you can, using a hose to get rid of the rest. The stems of dahlias are

hollow, and if moisture collects at the base of the stems while the tubers are being stored, it will cause them to rot. So turn the tubers and stems upside down and leave them for a couple of weeks in a cool, dry place to allow any moisture to drain from the stems. After that, box up the tubers in potting mix, making sure the crowns (the point where the stems meet the tubers) are not buried. Keep them in a cool, frost-free place over winter. They can be started back into growth in spring.

CONTAINERS

Create winter interest

A quick way to bring color and interest to your garden in winter is by planning your containers creatively—and you certainly don't need to stick to bedding plants. Many evergreen shrubs will provide color and interest year round. Variegated shrubs are particularly good value and will brighten up a dull or bare corner at any time of the year. There are many to choose from, but look out for *Euonymus japonicus* 'Marieke' and 'Aureopictus'. Varieties of variegated boxwood and dwarf conifers also come in a wide range of shapes and colors. Other plants to brighten up containers throughout the winter include hardy cyclamen and heathers, which also have a wide range of foliage hues. Winter-flowering pansies will give a bright, cheerful display from now right into the early summer.

TEN-MINUTE TASKS

- **Plant** spring-flowering bulbs this month and next (see page 136).
- **Prune** climbing roses and tie them in before autumn gales pick up.
- **Clear leaves** from around alpines to prevent rots and other diseases setting in.
- **Reseed** any bare or worn patches in lawns.

"""

October ushers in a richness of color, with a multitude of hues displayed by autumn foliage—and night frosts and clear, sunny days bring out the colors with even more intensity.

THE KITCHEN GARDEN

By October, you can really feel the change in seasons. Your main focus is clearing away and composting the remains of summer's harvest.

Prepare the soil and tidy beds

After the rush of harvest, October is a good time to get your plot in order. Clear away plant supports so that they don't rot over winter, and remove dead foliage. Dig over beds where the soil has become hard and compacted, pulling out any weeds. Then dig in green manures (see page 114) that won't overwinter.

Dry out beans for storage

If the weather is fair, leave any remaining bean pods on the plants to dry. If it's wet, cut them down and hang them up indoors or somewhere sheltered. When the beans are completely dried, pod and store them in airtight containers, ready to use in soups and casseroles.

HARVEST HIGHLIGHTS

Grapes

Midseason varieties are traditionally harvested in the middle of the month, and late-season varieties at the end—but let the weather dictate. If summer and autumn have been hot and sunny, grapes will be ready for picking earlier. If not, leave them on the vine as long as possible.

Parsnips

Traditionally, parsnips are not lifted until after a couple of frosts have concentrated and improved their flavor, so October may be your first chance to do so.

Raspberries

Autumn-fruiting raspberries should go on cropping until the arrival of the first serious frosts.

DON'T FORGET

- **Cover** late lettuce crops on cold nights.
- **Lift** and store carrots, turnips, and rutabagas.
- **Protect** celeriac crowns from frost with a mulch of dry straw.

1 *Rhus typhina*

15x20ft (5x6m); Zones 3–8

Also known as the staghorn sumac, this spreading deciduous tree has brilliant orange-red leaves in autumn.

GROW IT in any moist, well-drained soil. It tolerates light shade, but for the best autumn color, make sure it gets plenty of sun.

2 *Nerine bowdenii*

18x3in (45x8cm); Zones 7–11

In autumn, it bears rounded heads of funnel-shaped, faintly scented pink flowers. The strap-shaped leaves emerge after flowering.

GROW IT in full sun in sharply drained soil. Provide a dry winter mulch in cold areas. An ideal spot is at the base of a warm, sunny wall or in raised beds.

3 *Sorbus commixta*

30x22ft (10x7m); Zones 5–9

Commonly called mountain ash, this deciduous tree is festooned with clusters of orange-red berries in autumn, while the divided leaves turn from yellow to red and purple.

GROW IT in full sun or dappled shade in any fertile, moist, but well-drained neutral to acid soil.

4 *Acer palmatum* 'Corallinum'

6x10ft (2x3m); Zones 5–9

This small tree has green leaves in summer, which turn a striking red, orange, and yellow in autumn.

GROW IT in full sun or dappled shade in leafy, moist, but well-drained soil. Shelter from cold winds and spring frosts.

5 *Hesperantha coccinea* 'Sunrise'

24x12in (60x30cm); Zones 8–11

This hardy perennial bears spikes of glossy, salmon-pink flowers from late summer to early winter. They are good for cutting.

GROW IT in full sun in fertile, moist, but well-drained soil in mixed or herbaceous borders or in containers.

AT THEIR BEST

GET AHEAD

MAKE A VEGETABLE CLAMP

This traditional technique for insulating and storing root vegetables during the winter has stood the test of time — and for good reason. It's simple, inexpensive, and helps avoid food waste by enabling you to enjoy your crops well after the ground has frozen solid.

GOOD TO KNOW
_____

Potatoes, rutabagas, turnips, carrots, and beets can all be stored in a clamp.

1.

In a dry, sheltered spot, spread out an 8in- (20cm-) thick layer of clean straw and stack vegetables on top in a pyramid shape, with the largest roots at the bottom and necks (where the stem meets the tops) facing outward.

2.

Carefully cover the pyramid with more clean straw — at least 8in (20cm) to keep vegetables frost-free.

3.

If particularly cold weather is forecast, add a 6in (15cm) layer of soil to act as further insulation for the vegetables inside.

4.

Firm down the sides of the clamp, making it as stable as possible, and keep a close watch on it for any signs of attack by rodents.

MY GARDEN IN OCTOBER

NOVEMBER

This month can be damp and raw, though with any luck the rich autumn displays will continue into November. Either way, there can be no doubt that winter is now on its way, so make the most of any good weather.

KEY TASKS

- Wash any pots and trays once cleared of summer annuals.
- Clean out nesting boxes and put food out for the birds on a regular basis.
- Check for hibernating creatures before disturbing log piles or burning woody prunings that can't be composted.
- Insulate the greenhouse and install heaters if necessary.
- Plant bare-root trees, shrubs, and roses.
- Protect all tender and newly planted shrubs from frost and wind, and alpines from winter rain.
- Insulate pots that will remain outside during winter.
- Plant fruit trees and bushes, and winter-prune established plants.

LAST CHANCE

November is your last opportunity to lift and store dahlias before the weather gets too cold (see pages 124–125).

AROUND THE GARDEN

Flowers may be scarce in the garden, but berries, evergreen foliage, and trees with decorative bark can add interest on the dull, cold days. You can warm yourself up by cleaning up the garden.

GENERAL CARE

Clean out bird boxes

Attracting birds into the garden is a crucial way to help replace disappearing rural habitats—and your new feathered friends will repay the favor in their own way by eating slugs and snails. To encourage birds to use boxes year after year, clear out old nesting material in the autumn. Do this as soon as possible, as birds will soon be looking for winter roosts. If they are already familiar with a box by spring, they are more likely to select it as a nesting site.

Protect young plants from rabbits

For relatively small mammals, rabbits can do a lot of damage. A few simple precautions can prevent the worst of it. Surround young plants and tree trunks with chicken wire, or wrap special rabbit guards directly around the trunks to stop rabbits from eating the bark. For especially valuable sites, like vegetable beds, consider putting chicken wire around the perimeter, sinking it at least 6in (15cm) into the ground, with the bottom few inches bent outward. In your efforts, be careful not to deter other wildlife, such as chipmunks, which may be on the lookout for places to hibernate. A log pile will be a welcome home for these creatures.

Insulate cold frames

If you don't have a greenhouse, cold frames are endlessly useful. At this time of year, they can be used to protect young or tender plants from the cooler weather. They will withstand mild frosts, but as winter sets in, it can be well worth adding a little more protection. Insulating cold frames with reused bubble wrap or styrofoam slabs will help keep out several degrees of frost, enabling you to overwinter some tender plants there. On very cold nights, add more protection by covering the frame with an old rug.

TREES, SHRUBS, AND CLIMBERS

Protect tender and newly planted trees and shrubs

Depending on which zone you live in, you may not have had a frost—but that doesn't mean it's too early to start protecting your trees and shrubs. Strong winds in cold temperatures can cause more harm to plants than a severe frost on its own, while bitter winds damage foliage by causing dehydration. Construct a windbreak from posts and netting, and prioritize evergreen shrubs and hedging plants over deciduous ones. Smaller shrubs and those that are newly planted can be protected from frost by packing straw or pine needles around them, held in place with netting.

Begin winter-pruning deciduous trees and shrubs

Now is the time to remove dead, diseased, and damaged wood from most deciduous trees. Although pruning creates wounds, which are potential entry points for disease, it is less risky than leaving the unhealthy wood on the plant. Any further cuts you make will probably be more cosmetic, but consider the effect before removing anything substantial: it's not only the effect of removing growth that you must envision, but also the direction in which the new growth that will come from the point of pruning will grow.

While hacking away at woody growth is a satisfying job, don't prune unless the plant really needs it. Unnecessary pruning weakens growth, and the more wounds you make the more vulnerable the tree is to disease. The fungal disease silver leaf, for example, usually infects through wounds caused by pruning in winter, so it may be wise to delay pruning susceptible trees, such as ornamental cherries, until the summer.

PERENNIALS, ANNUALS, BULBS, AND BEDDING

Cut back ornamental grasses and bamboos

Any grasses that aren't taking center stage in winter are best cut back now, as they can often look messy when it isn't their peak season. Some bamboos, if their canes are thick enough, can be cut, cleaned up, and stored and used for supporting plants next season. You can also thin out ornamental canes on bamboos, so that congested clumps are opened up and the canes are displayed to their best advantage.

Protect seedlings of hardy annuals

Keep an eye on the weather forecast and, if it turns very cold, protect those hardy annuals sown earlier in the autumn. Cover them with cloches, or have some fleece handy to throw over the plants. It would be rare indeed for these plants to be killed by frost, but it does no harm to have some protection to hand for really severe weather.

Plant tulip bulbs

If you haven't planted all your spring-flowering bulbs yet, be sure to do so now. Now is also the best time to plant tulips to avoid the bulbs being infected with the fungal disease tulip fire. Try to get them in before the end of the month. Tulips flower

better in a sunny position. If your soil is heavy clay, lighten it by digging in coarse sand. You can, of course, grow tulips in pots too. One advantage of growing them in pots is that they can be planted, pot and all, in any part of the garden lacking color in the spring. They are easily lifted out again when the flowers are over. Plant tulips in borders and pots just as you would other bulbs, at two to three times their own depth. Plant the bulbs on a layer of coarse sand to prevent them from rotting off. If in doubt, it is always better to plant tulips a little more deeply than too near the surface.

CONTAINERS

Insulate outdoor pots

Bring as many planted containers under cover as you can; the roots of plants growing in containers outside tend to be more prone to suffering from frost damage than plants that are growing in the open ground. Any pots that are too large will need some protection. Insulate them by wrapping burlap sacks securely around the pots, and tie up the leaves of plants such as cordylines to protect the growing tip from excess winter wet, which will rot it, and wrap in fleece. Containers can also be moved together for mutual protection. Modern terracotta containers are generally frost-proof, but older pots may not be, so even if they are empty, wrap them or take them indoors for the winter months. Lift containers off the ground a little to improve their drainage, too. You can even buy decorative "feet" from garden centers for this very purpose.

TEN-MINUTE TASKS

- **Check** all stored bulbs, corms, and tubers, and throw away any that are showing signs of rotting.
- **Tie in** long shoots of climbers and wall shrubs to prevent them from being damaged in bad weather.
- **Clear** any leaves that have accumulated on top of clumps of perennials.
- **Cover** vulnerable alpines to protect the crowns from rain, or take alpines in pots under cover.

"

Many people regard November as the end of the gardening season, but it is really the beginning. Work done now is the crucial backstage preparation for the garden's performance to start next spring.

THE KITCHEN GARDEN

The gluts of summer are long behind us, but there's still plenty you can do to keep your patch moving along until the spring.

Assess your soil

November is a good time to check on your soil. Before the ground becomes too wet, test its pH value (see page 8). If it's too acidic, spread some powdered lime over the surface and rake it in—brassicas in particular prefer alkaline soils. Don't add lime at the same time as manure, though.

Remove nets from fruit cages

It might go against the grain, but at this time of year, you actually want birds in your fruit cages. Take off nets to allow birds in to pick off insects and their eggs. You'll still want to net Brussels sprouts, cabbages, and other brassicas, though.

HARVEST HIGHLIGHTS

Cranberries

Pick the berries when their color darkens to a rich, deep red. They should last on the bush until you need them.

Green beans

Beans intended for drying may be left on the plants until the pods have completely dried out.

Spinach

Winter spinach varieties are fast-growing and bred to tolerate shorter days; they should crop this month. Provide extra protection in severe weather.

DON'T FORGET

- **Make** leaf mold (see page 122).
- **Check** stored fruit and vegetables and discard any that show signs of rot.
- **Weed** beds, then dig in manure and compost.

1 *Vitis coignetiae*

50ft (15m) tall; spread indefinite; Zones 6–9

This vigorous climber is undoubtedly at its best in the autumn when the large, heart-shaped leaves turn gold, then brilliant red and purple.

GROW IT in sun or partial shade in well-drained, preferably neutral to slightly alkaline, soil. Prune in winter and again in summer, as needed, to confine it to its allotted space.

2 *Iris foetidissima*

3x3ft (90x90cm); Zones 6–9

The stinking iris flowers in early summer, but its truly show-stopping moment comes in autumn with its vivid scarlet seeds.

GROW IT in sun or shade in any well-drained soil. It's ideal for dry, shady borders.

3 *Actaea matsumurae* 'White Pearl'

36x24in (90x60cm); Zones 4–9

From early to mid-autumn, this herbaceous perennial bears spires of white flowers that open from green buds.

GROW IT in moist, fertile, humus-rich soil in partial shade in damp borders or woodland gardens.

4 *Chelone obliqua*

24x12in (60x30cm); Zones 5–9

From late summer to mid-autumn, this plant bears dark-pink or purple flowers with yellow beards on the lower lip.

GROW IT in full sun or partial shade in deep, fertile soil that retains moisture. Mulch well in spring before growth begins.

5 *Chrysanthemum* 'Glowing Lynn'

18x18in (45x45cm) or more; Zones 4–10

In late summer and autumn, this chrysanthemum bears masses of double, red-bronze flowers, which make excellent cut flowers.

GROW IT in full sun in fertile, well-drained soil. Except in very cold areas, it can be left outdoors in winter—but be sure to protect the crown with a deep, dry mulch.

AT THEIR BEST

GET AHEAD

PLANT NEW ROSES

November is your first opportunity to buy bare-root roses, which should be available from now through March. They might not look like much yet, but it's always best to buy bare-root and plant now if you can. You'll get better results than more expensive container-grown shrubs bought and planted next spring.

GOOD TO KNOW

Before you buy bare-root plants, make sure the root systems have been lifted with care and haven't dried up. You can also plant trees using the technique shown here.

1.

Locate and prepare your planting area. If you are planting new roses to replace old ones, take out as much of the old soil as possible and replace it with soil from a part of the garden where roses haven't grown. This is to avoid "rose sickness."

2.

Cultivate as large an area as you can, or dig as large a hole as possible, and work in plenty of organic matter. Never allow the roots to dry out; if your roses have arrived by mail order and the roots are dry, put them in a bucket of water first.

3.

Plant the rose deep enough so that the point at which it was grafted is about 2in (5cm) below ground level. Work soil in among the roots well and firm as you go.

4.

Mulch the surface with well-rotted garden compost or manure.

....
....
....
....
....
....
....
....
....
....
....
....
....
....
....
....
....
....
....
....
....

DECEMBER

Sunny days in December can be truly invigorating. If you bundle up well, there is nothing stopping you from having a good day in the garden, digging or catching up with other clearing or maintenance jobs.

KEY TASKS

- Prevent ponds, water features, and bird baths from freezing.
- Continue winter digging, incorporating organic matter.
- Repair lawns, sheds, and fences when the weather allows.
- Protect all plants that are vulnerable to frost.
- Reduce watering of plants that are overwintering under cover.
- Lift and heel in celery so that you have plenty of winter supplies, and earth up tall Brussels sprout stems to support them.
- Spray fruit trees and roses with a plant oil winter wash to reduce pest and disease problems.

LAST CHANCE

By December, many zones run the risk of a hard frost, so make sure you've protected any plants and pots that might be vulnerable.

145

AROUND THE GARDEN

When wintery weather isn't keeping you inside, there's plenty to do in the garden. And keep an eye out for company: you may spot a robin or cardinal following your progress.

GENERAL CARE

Move plants

Any notes you've taken during the year will come into their own this month. Check deciduous trees, shrubs, climbers, and herbaceous perennials: if any are growing in the wrong place or have become too big for their current spot, now is a good time to move them—if soil conditions permit. Always take as big a root ball as you can when lifting larger plants, and revitalize the soil the plant was taken from and in its new position. Stake tall plants to prevent wind rock and provide a windbreak shelter.

Make use of woody prunings

Winter is a prime time to prune trees and shrubs (see page 135), not least because it's easier to see what you're doing with no leaves in the way! (Check the recommended pruning times for your trees first, though; some fruit trees, such as plums, are better left until spring or summer to avoid the risk of silver leaf disease.) Consider shredding rather than burning prunings. They make a great mulch or can be added to the compost heap. If your garden is mostly shrubs and lawn, keep a pile of shreddings to mix with grass clippings in summer. They need plenty of air to rot down properly. Don't shred any diseased material or the disease will spread.

Insulate outside taps

When ice forms in freezing temperatures, water expands and this can easily burst pipes. Insulate taps by binding them in several layers of burlap, or use specialized products. If possible, turn off the supply to outside taps and drain the pipe in winter.

TREES, SHRUBS, AND CLIMBERS

Mind the gaps

December is a good time to cast an eye over hedges, shrubberies, and other such areas to check for gaps and think about how to fill them. You might want to order bare-root shrubs, or—if you've taken cuttings earlier in the year—prepare to use those instead.

Shape overgrown deciduous hedges

No matter how often we trim hedges like beech and hornbeam through the summer, they creep imperceptibly outward, taking up more space and becoming more difficult to cut. Now—when the plants are dormant and there is no chance of disturbing nesting birds—is a good time to reduce the hedge to a manageable size. On an old, established hedge you may need loppers or a pruning saw to cut some of the larger branches. Cut back the sides until the hedge is no more than 18–24in (45–60cm) wide at the top, tapering it so that the bottom of the hedge is wider. This shaping will protect the hedge from damage by heavy snowfalls. The top can be trimmed to whatever height you want. To get the top level, you may need to put up a line at the height required. Shred prunings to add them to compost or for a useful mulch (see opposite).

Prune ornamental vines

Vines can produce growths up to 10ft (3m) or more in one season, so if they are not pruned over several years, you may end up with a mess! Thin out any overcrowded shoots, then prune side shoots to two buds from the main stems kept as a framework.

PERENNIALS, ANNUALS, BULBS, AND BEDDING

Keep perennials clear of leaves

Any leaves that have accumulated on top of clumps of perennials should be removed. If the leaves are left there for any length of time, the plants will suffer through lack of light, and the dark, moist conditions will attract slugs and snails. Don't burn the fallen leaves; you can either add them to the compost heap or make a separate leaf heap to make leaf mold (see page 122).

Plan borders and color schemes

Even on a cold winter day, you can dream of the summer to come. It's exciting to try some new plant varieties each year, and by ordering early you have the best chance of getting the varieties you want and having them in good time for sowing. Many people leave it until the last minute to order their seeds and get caught up in the rush of spring orders to seed companies.

TEN-MINUTE TASKS

- **Check** whether newly planted trees and shrubs have been loosened by winds or lifted by frost. If you see cracks around the plant, gently firm in with your feet.
- **Shake** snow off trees and shrubs.
- **Cut** a few shoots from winter jasmine in early December. Put the shoots in water, and keep them in a cool place indoors. The buds will begin to open, and you'll be able to use these beautifully scented flowers in your Christmas decorations.

CONTAINERS

Clean up permanent plants in containers

Check over permanent plants regularly and clear away any debris. Fallen leaves in the base of plants in containers don't just look unsightly; they encourage disease and give pests somewhere to hibernate.

Move pots of half-hardy plants inside

Even plants that are borderline hardy are vulnerable in the harshest weather, and those growing in containers are more at risk because their roots are above the ground. Make sure you move these plants inside now. Even in the warmer areas of the country, there can be frosts in December, so it's safest to move plants into an unheated or cool greenhouse or conservatory. Very little heat is required; otherwise, the plants may put on too much growth, which will be very straggly due to the lack of light. Water the plants carefully, giving them enough to keep them alive. Don't overdo it, though, as too much water can kill plants off. It's also worth being aware that damp, still air can encourage diseases, such as botrytis. Whenever possible, ensure that there is plenty of air circulating around the plants, and open the ventilators on reasonably mild days.

POTTING LILIES

You can start potting lilies a little earlier in the year, but for a succession of blooms, you'll want to keep doing so well into December. Put four or five bulbs into a 7in (18cm) pot containing peat-free growing medium mixed with some sand, covering the bulbs by about 4in (10cm). Water them, and leave the pots outside to allow a good root system to form. When new growth starts in the spring, either take some pots inside and the lilies will flower early, or leave them out and wait for the flowers to emerge in spring.

" "

December can be a wonderful month in the garden. The days may be short, but on the whole the weather may not be too bad, with wonderfully clear, frosty, sunny days, when it can be a pleasure to be out.

THE KITCHEN GARDEN

December may not be as lean a month as you'd expect, with winter brassicas at their peak. Besides that, it's time to prepare for next year.

Cover beds

As long as the earth isn't already waterlogged, it's not too late to spread sheets or even old rugs over the soil in order to keep off heavy rain, suppress weeds, and help warm the ground to make it ready for early sowing and planting next year.

Check wires and ties

Inspect all stakes, wires, and ties on your fruit trees and bushes. Replace any that are worn or broken, loosen any that are too tight, and ensure that others are secure.

Lift root vegetables for storage

Harvest the last of your carrots, turnips, kohlrabi, and any remaining beets. They can be stored if necessary (see page 130). Celeriac and parsnips can stay in the ground if there's no risk of their being "frozen in," although a mulch of straw or pine needles will help protect them.

HARVEST HIGHLIGHTS

Brussels sprouts

These festive favorites should be plentiful now. Harvest one by one, starting at the bottom of each stem, or uproot the stalks whole: they'll keep for a few days in a bucket of water.

Jerusalem artichokes

Dig up the last of your Jerusalem artichokes this month. Unless you want another crop next year, search out and remove all the tubers.

Rutabagas

Although rutabagas may be left in the ground until the end of December, beyond that they tend to become woody. It's better to lift them all now and, if necessary, store them.

DON'T FORGET

- **Weed** and mulch carefully around all established fruit trees, bushes, and canes.
- **Remove** dying leaves from brassicas as soon as they start to turn yellow.

1 *Rhododendron* 'Inga'

20x20in (50x50cm); Zones 4–8

In winter, this compact azalea bears funnel-shaped, pink flowers with white margins on slightly frilled petals.

GROW IT in pots of lime-free (ericaceous) growing medium in bright light, but shaded from direct sun.

2 *Jasminum nudiflorum*

10x10ft (3x3m); Zones 6–9

Masses of bright-yellow flowers bloom on this plant's bare branches in winter and early spring.

GROW IT in any fertile garden soil, tied into supports on a sunny or lightly shaded wall or sprawling over a sunny bank.

3 *Viburnum* x *bodnantense* 'Dawn'

10x6ft (3x2m); Zones 5–7

From late autumn to early spring, this deciduous shrub bears small, rounded clusters of fragrant pink flowers on bare branches.

GROW IT in any reasonably fertile, well-drained soil in sun or dappled shade. It is ideal for shrub borders, woodland gardens, or informal hedging.

4 *Mahonia* x *media* 'Charity'

15x12ft (5x4m); Zones 6–9

This evergreen shrub brightens up the garden with honey-scented flowers all the way from late autumn to early spring.

GROW IT in moist but well-drained, humus-rich soil in partial shade or in full sun, if soil is reliably moist.

5 *Aucuba japonica* 'Variegata'

Up to 10x10ft (3x3m); Zones 6–9

The female plant's variegated leaves get extra interest in winter, with bright red berries.

GROW IT in almost any conditions, but it is especially good in dark, shady corners. Avoid waterlogged soil.

GET AHEAD

PRUNE APPLE AND PEAR TREES

You can prune established, freestanding apple and pear trees any time from now until February, when the trees are dormant, and it's a good task to check off during this fairly quiet month. Pruning might seem intimidating, but it shouldn't be. Your aims are quite simple: cut out dead, diseased, or damaged wood; remove overcrowded branches; and stimulate growth. Trained trees or trees grown as columns and cordons are pruned in summer.

GOOD TO KNOW

Use clean, sharp tools to avoid damaging the tree and spreading disease. Make cuts as clean as you can, trimming off ragged edges, and angle them so that the face of the wound slopes gently downward to allow rain to drain off.

1.

Remove branches growing in toward the middle of the tree to allow air to circulate freely. Use a pruning saw to cut them back to the "collar" where they join a main stem.

2.

Shorten by a half or a third any branches that are too long. Cut them back to a side branch that faces outward. Make two cuts: the first from underneath, halfway through; and a second from above to join the first.

3.

Remove old, tired branches and thin out some of the recent, new growth by cutting back to shorter, outward-facing stems or short spurs.

4.

Cut out any new shoots and stems that have sprouted from around the wounds of previous pruning cuts. They are unlikely ever to fruit.

MY GARDEN IN DECEMBER

CROP PLANNER

This schedule applies best to USDA Zones 6–8. Depending on your location, you may need to adjust dates by as much as a month either way. Check with your local garden center or state Agriculture Extension Service for specific recommendations.

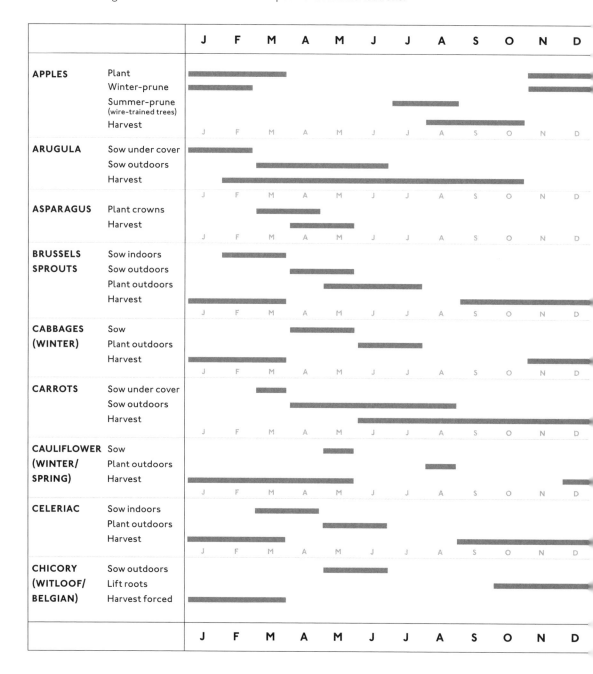

		J	F	M	A	M	J	J	A	S	O	N	D
APPLES	Plant	■	■	■	■							■	■
	Winter-prune	■	■									■	■
	Summer-prune (wire-trained trees)							■	■				
	Harvest								■	■	■		
ARUGULA	Sow under cover	■	■										
	Sow outdoors			■	■	■	■	■					
	Harvest	■	■	■	■	■	■	■	■	■	■		
ASPARAGUS	Plant crowns			■	■								
	Harvest				■	■							
BRUSSELS SPROUTS	Sow indoors		■	■									
	Sow outdoors				■	■							
	Plant outdoors					■	■	■					
	Harvest	■	■	■						■	■	■	■
CABBAGES (WINTER)	Sow				■	■							
	Plant outdoors						■	■					
	Harvest	■	■	■								■	■
CARROTS	Sow under cover			■									
	Sow outdoors				■	■	■	■	■				
	Harvest						■	■	■	■	■	■	■
CAULIFLOWER (WINTER/SPRING)	Sow					■							
	Plant outdoors								■				
	Harvest	■	■	■	■								■
CELERIAC	Sow indoors			■	■								
	Plant outdoors					■	■						
	Harvest	■	■	■						■	■	■	■
CHICORY (WITLOOF/ BELGIAN)	Sow outdoors					■	■						
	Lift roots										■	■	
	Harvest forced	■	■	■									

	J	F	M	A	M	J	J	A	S	O	N	D
CHILES & PEPPERS												
Sow indoors			■	■								
Plant outdoors					■	■						
Harvest							■	■	■	■		
CRANBERRIES												
Plant			■	■	■	■			■	■	■	
Trim			■	■							■	
Harvest									■	■	■	
EGGPLANT												
Sow indoors			■	■								
Plant outdoors					■	■						
Harvest							■	■	■	■		
GRAPES												
Plant		■	■	■	■					■	■	
Winter-prune	■										■	■
Summer-prune					■	■	■					
Harvest									■	■		
GREEN BEANS												
Sow indoors				■	■							
Sow under cover					■							
Sow outdoors					■	■						
Plant outdoors						■						
Harvest							■	■	■	■	■	
JERUSALEM ARTICHOKES												
Plant tubers outdoors		■	■	■	■							
Harvest	■	■									■	■
KALE												
Sow indoors				■	■	■						
Sow outdoors					■	■	■					
Plant outdoors						■	■	■				
Harvest	■	■	■	■							■	■
LEEKS												
Sow indoors	■	■										
Sow outdoors		■	■	■								
Plant outdoors					■	■						
Harvest	■	■	■	■	■				■	■	■	■
LETTUCE												
Sow indoors		■	■	■								
Sow under cover			■	■	■				■			
Sow outdoors				■	■	■	■	■				
Plant outdoors				■	■	■						
Harvest			■	■	■	■	■	■	■	■	■	■

		J	F	M	A	M	J	J	A	S	O	N	D
ONIONS	Sow indoors	▓	▓										
	Sow outdoors			▓	▓				▓				
	Transplant			▓	▓								
	Plant sets outdoors			▓	▓					▓	▓		
	Harvest						▓	▓	▓	▓			
PARSNIPS	Sow outdoors			▓	▓								
	Harvest	▓	▓	▓								▓	▓
PEACHES & NECTARINES	Plant									▓	▓	▓	▓
	Prune			▓	▓	▓	▓	▓	▓	▓			
	Harvest							▓	▓	▓			
PEAS	Sow indoors	▓	▓									▓	▓
	Sow under cover		▓								▓	▓	
	Sow outdoors			▓	▓	▓	▓						
	Plant outdoors			▓	▓	▓							
	Harvest					▓	▓	▓	▓	▓	▓		
POLE BEANS	Sow indoors				▓	▓							
	Sow under cover					▓							
	Sow outdoors					▓	▓						
	Plant outdoors					▓							
	Harvest						▓	▓	▓	▓	▓		
POTATOES	Plant			▓	▓	▓							
	Harvest					▓	▓	▓	▓	▓			
RADISHES (SUMMER)	Sow indoors	▓	▓										
	Sow under cover			▓									
	Sow outdoors				▓	▓	▓	▓	▓	▓			
	Plant outdoors			▓									
	Harvest				▓	▓	▓	▓	▓	▓	▓	▓	
RASPBERRIES (FALL)	Plant	▓	▓	▓									
	Prune		▓	▓									
	Harvest								▓	▓	▓	▓	
RHUBARB	Sow indoors		▓										
	Transplant				▓	▓							
	Plant sets outdoors	▓	▓	▓							▓	▓	▓
	Harvest			▓	▓	▓	▓						

Crop	Activity	J	F	M	A	M	J	J	A	S	O	N	D
RUTABAGAS	Sow outdoors					■	■						
	Harvest	■	■							■	■	■	■
SPINACH	Sow indoors	■	■										
	Sow outdoors			■	■	■	■		■	■			
	Plant outdoors			■									
	Harvest				■	■	■	■	■	■	■	■	
SPRING ONIONS	Sow outdoors			■	■	■	■	■	■				
	Harvest			■	■	■	■	■	■				
SPROUTING BROCCOLI	Sow indoors		■	■	■	■							
	Sow outdoors			■	■	■	■	■					
	Transplant under cover			■	■								
	Plant outdoors					■	■	■	■				
	Harvest	■	■				■	■	■	■	■	■	
SQUASHES (WINTER)	Sow indoors				■	■							
	Sow outdoors						■						
	Plant outdoors					■	■						
	Harvest								■	■	■		
STRAWBERRIES (SUMMER)	Plant			■	■	■	■	■	■	■			
	Harvest					■	■	■					
SWISS CHARD	Sow outdoors				■	■	■	■	■				
	Harvest			■	■	■	■	■	■	■	■	■	
TOMATOES	Sow indoors		■	■	■								
	Plant outdoors					■	■						
	Harvest							■	■	■	■		
TURNIPS	Sow under cover		■	■	■								
	Sow outdoors				■	■	■	■	■				
	Harvest					■	■	■	■	■	■	■	■
ZUCCHINI	Sow indoors				■	■							
	Sow outdoors												
	Plant outdoors					■	■						
	Harvest							■	■	■	■		

ABOUT THE ILLUSTRATOR

Originally from Newcastle-upon-Tyne, England, Alice Pattullo lives and works in East London. Her illustrations are regularly commissioned for editorial, publishing, and packaging projects. Alice also develops original limited edition screen prints for sale and exhibition in the UK. For this work, she is often inspired by British traditions, folklore, and superstitions.

For my mum, Mandy.

Project Editor Amy Slack
US Editor Lori Hand
Senior Designer Barbara Zuniga
Production Editor David Almond
Senior Production Controller Stephanie McConnell
Jackets Coordinator Jasmin Lennie
Editorial Manager Ruth O'Rourke
Design Manager Marianne Markham
Art Director Maxine Pedliham
Publisher Katie Cowan

Editor Alice Horne
Proofreader Francesco Piscitelli
US consultant John Tullock
Designer Christine Keilty
Design Concept Giulia Garbin
Illustrator Alice Pattullo
Consultant Gardening Publisher Chris Young

First American Edition, 2022
Published in the United States by DK Publishing
1745 Broadway, 20th Floor, New York, NY 10019

Artwork copyright © 2022 Alice Pattullo

Text in this book has been adapted from material featured in
Gardening Through the Year and *The Kitchen Garden.*

Copyright © 2022 Dorling Kindersley Limited
DK, a Division of Penguin Random House LLC
22 23 24 25 26 10 9 8 7 6 5 4 3 2 1
001–333845–Sept/2022

A catalog record for this book is available
from the Library of Congress.
ISBN 978-0-7440-7368-3

Printed and bound in Slovakia

For the curious

www.dk.com

MIX
Paper from
responsible sources
FSC™ C018179
www.fsc.org

This book was made with Forest Stewardship Council ™ certified paper—one small step in DK's commitment to a sustainable future. For more information go to www.dk.com/our-green-pledge